Reading Engagement
Grade 7

By
JANET P. SITTER, Ph.D.

COPYRIGHT © 2005 Mark Twain Media, Inc.

ISBN 1-58037-291-0

Printing No. CD-404018

Mark Twain Media, Inc., Publishers
Distributed by Carson-Dellosa Publishing Company, Inc.

Table of Contents

Introduction

The goal of *Reading Engagement: Grade 7* is to help students improve their reading comprehension skills. The reading selections and reading guides in this book have been developed to provide instructional reading practice for below-average and/or reluctant readers, to provide independent reading activities for the average reader, and to provide supplemental reading for the more competent readers in your classroom. By completing the readings and activities in *Reading Engagement: Grade 7,* your students will receive instruction, practice, and/or reinforcement in these strategies routinely practiced by good readers:

1. Good readers see reading as a comprehension process, not a decoding process.
2. Good readers relate what they are reading to what they already know.
3. Good readers decode rapidly, applying a number of word analysis skills to figure out unknown words.
4. Good readers know and recognize more words and have larger vocabularies.
5. Good readers monitor their comprehension and take action when they don't understand what they are reading.

Reading Engagement: Grade 7 uses interesting text to focus students' motivation and interest on what they are reading. The activities in the reading guides help students make connections between what they are reading and what they already know. The vocabulary exercises help students not only build vocabulary but learn new words in meaningful ways. The comprehension questions seek to improve the thinking skills of students by asking questions at the literal, interpretive, and applied levels of critical thinking. The reading guides provide support for comprehension before reading, during reading, and after reading. The student's comprehension is tested through simple, informal reading assessments following each reading. And finally, each lesson contains an activity to extend the student's understanding after reading.

Each lesson is designed for independent student use, though with reluctant or below-average readers, instruction might be necessary. Each lesson is independent of all the other lessons and increases in difficulty as the student moves through them. Each lesson can be treated as a unit of instruction and can become part of the student's reading portfolio.

The more students read, the better readers they become. These readings are designed to help them become better readers.

How to Use This Book

The reading lessons in this book are divided into four levels. Each level increases the difficulty of the reading, beginning with Level One, Lesson 1 at a fifth grade reading level and continuing with incremental jumps in reading difficulty culminating in Level Four, Lesson 3 at an eighth-grade reading level.

Level One	Level Two	Level Three	Level Four
Lesson 1 5.2	Lesson 1 6.5	Lesson 1 6.9	Lesson 1 7.3
Lesson 2 5.7	Lesson 2 6.6	Lesson 2 7.0	Lesson 2 8.2
Lesson 3 5.8	Lesson 3 6.6	Lesson 3 7.0	Lesson 3 8.5
	Lesson 4 6.7	Lesson 4 7.1	

Each lesson contains a short 300–1,000 word story with a reading guide. The instructional framework for the Reading Guides consists of activities to do before reading the selection, during the reading of the selection, and after reading the selection.

BEFORE READING

The activities in the Before Reading section of the Reading Guides are intended to prepare the reader for the reading by:

       a.   establishing a purpose for reading;
       b.   building and activating background knowledge;
       c.   connecting what is known to what is to be learned;
       d.   presenting key concepts and vocabulary; and
       e.   activating student interest and motivation.

DURING READING

The activities in the During Reading section of the Reading Guides are intended to support the reader during the reading by:

       a.   encouraging readers to read actively;
       b.   guiding interactions between readers and text;
       c.   using questions to activate critical thinking; and
       d.   checking and expanding student comprehension skills.

How to Use This Book (cont.)

AFTER READING

The activities in the After Reading section of the Reading Guides are intended to assess and extend the reader's comprehension by:

a.   promoting thoughtful consideration of the text;
d.   supporting the reader's comprehension with Internet experiences;
b.   checking and evaluating the reader's comprehension; and
c.   extending the reader's understanding of the text.

Reading comprehension skills refer to a wide range of skills readers use to get meaning from text. While these skills develop over time, the lessons in *Reading Engagement: Grade 7* provide instruction, practice, and reinforcement in the following skills.

- Identifying details
- Stating main idea
- Inferring main idea
- Recalling details
- Inferring details
- Inferring cause and effect
- Following directions
- Determining sequence
- Locating reference
- Recalling information
- Summarizing ideas
- Identifying time sequence
- Retelling in own words
- Inferring author's purpose/intent

- Comparing and contrasting
- Drawing conclusions
- Making generalizations
- Recognizing structure and organization of text
- Predicting outcomes
- Evaluating text
- Judging author's qualifications
- Distinguishing facts from opinions
- Recognizing figurative language
- Identifying mood
- Understanding mental imagery
- Recognizing signal words
- Recognizing elements of story

Reading Level Analysis for Reading Selections

Sample Begins: Did You Know…?
Sample Ends: • The Mona Lisa has no eyebrows.
Words: 585
Syllables: 823
Monosyllabic Words: 422
Words of 3 or more Syllables: 51
Sentences: 48
Syllables/Word: 1.42
Syllables/100 Words: 141.03
Monosyllabic Words/100 Words: 70.33
Polysyllabic Words/100 Words: 8.64
Sentences/100 Words: 8.14
Words/Sentence: 12.19
Reading Grade Level: 5.2

Sample Begins: Deep Sea Squid
Sample Ends: in the deep blue sea!
Words: 334
Syllables: 472
Monosyllabic Words: 233
Words of 3 or more Syllables: 31
Sentences: 18
Syllables/Word: 1.42
Syllables/100 Words: 141.32
Monosyllabic Words/100 Words: 69.77
Polysyllabic Words/100 Words: 9.29
Sentences/100 Words: 5.39
Words/Sentence: 18.56
Reading Grade Level: 5.7

Sample Begins: Delicious Mistakes
Sample Ends: ideas were the result.
Words: 684
Syllables: 1,044
Monosyllabic Words: 459
Words of 3 or more Syllables: 102
Sentences: 49
Syllables/Word: 1.53
Syllables/100 Words: 152.64
Monosyllabic Words/100 Words: 67.11

Polysyllabic Words/100 Words: 14.92
Sentences/100 Words: 7.17
Words/Sentence: 13.96
Reading Grade Level: 5.8

Sample Begins: Totally Absurd Inventions … for Pets!
Sample Ends: Sha-zamm!
Words: 635
Difficult Words (Dale-Chall): 97
Sentences: 69
Sentences/100 Words: 10.87
Words/Sentence: 9.21
% of Words not on the Dale-Chall List: 15.28
Reading Grade Level: 6.5

Sample Begins: Go for Broke!
Sample Ends: lost their lives.
Words: 675
Syllables: 1,116
Monosyllabic Words: 406
Words of 3 or more Syllables: 119
Sentences: 40
Syllables/Word: 1.66
Syllables/100 Words: 165.34
Monosyllabic Words/100 Words: 60.15
Polysyllabic Words/100 Words: 17.63
Sentences/100 Words: 5.93
Words/Sentence: 16.88
Reading Grade Level: 6.6

Sample Begins: Bill of Rights, Part I
Sample Ends: does not justify the means.
Words: 989
Syllables: 1,623
Monosyllabic Words: 607
Words of 3 or more Syllables: 190
Sentences: 56
Syllables/Word: 1.65
Syllables/100 Words: 164.11
Monosyllabic Words/100 Words: 61.38

Polysyllabic Words/100 Words: 19.22
Sentences/100 Words: 5.67
Words/Sentence: 17.67
Reading Grade Level: 6.6

Sample Begins: Bill of Rights, Part II
Sample Ends: a democratic government.
Words: 675
Syllables: 1,134
Monosyllabic Words: 414
Words of 3 or more Syllables: 149
Sentences: 42
Syllables/Word: 1.69
Syllables/100 Words: 168.01
Monosyllabic Words/100 Words: 61.34
Polysyllabic Words/100 Words: 22.08
Sentences/100 Words: 6.23
Words/Sentence: 16.08
Reading Grade Level: 6.7

Sample Begins: Baseball's Hall of Fame
Sample Ends: a popular tourist attraction!
Words: 434
Syllables: 733
Monosyllabic Words: 260
Words of 3 or more Syllables: 92
Sentences: 23
Syllables/Word: 1.69
Syllables/100 Words: 168.90
Monosyllabic Words/100 Words: 59.91
Polysyllabic Words/100 Words: 21.20
Sentences/100 Words: 5.30
Words/Sentence: 18.87
Reading Grade Level: 6.9

Reading Level Analysis for Reading Selections (cont.)

Sample Begins: Habitat for Humanity
Sample Ends:eliminate homelessness in America.
Words: 556
Syllables: 970
Monosyllabic Words: 310
Words of 3 or more Syllables: 115
Sentences: 33
Syllables/Word: 1.75
Syllables/100 Words: 174.47
Monosyllabic Words/100 Words: 55.76
Polysyllabic Words/100 Words: 20.69
Sentences/100 Words: 5.94
Words/Sentence: 16.85
Reading Grade Level: 7.0

Sample Begins: Harlem USA
Sample Ends: neighborhood known as Harlem.
Words: 563
Syllables: 992
Monosyllabic Words: 322
Words of 3 or more Syllables: 111
Sentences: 36
Syllables/Word: 1.77
Syllables/100 Words: 176.20
Monosyllabic Words/100 Words: 57.20
Polysyllabic Words/100 Words: 19.72
Sentences/100 Words: 6.40
Words/Sentence: 15.64
Reading Grade Level: 7.0

Sample Begins: The Gentle Giant
Sample Ends: to all who knew him.
Words: 726
Difficult Words (Dale-Chall): 129
Sentences: 55
Sentences/100 Words: 7.58
Words/Sentence: 13.21
% of Words not on the Dale-Chall List: 17.77
Reading Grade Level: 7.1

Sample Begins: Life in the Desert
Sample Ends: pistachio trees, and shrubs.
Words: 863
Difficult Words (Dale-Chall): 165
Sentences: 70
Sentences/100 Words: 8.12
Words/Sentence: 12.33
% of Words not on the Dale-Chall List: 19.12
Reading Grade Level: 7.3

Sample Begins: Tuskegee Airmen
Sample Ends: for other African-Americans.
Words: 478
Difficult Words (Dale-Chall): 115
Sentences: 33
Sentences/100 Words: 6.91
Words/Sentence: 14.49
% of Words not on the Dale-Chall List: 24.06
Reading Grade Level: 8.2

Sample Begins: The Choctaw
Sample Ends: strong and self-sufficient community.
Words: 535
Difficult Words (Dale-Chall): 134
Sentences: 30
Sentences/100 Words: 5.61
Words/Sentence: 17.84
% of Words not on the Dale-Chall List: 25.05
Reading Grade Level: 8.5

Name: _____ Date: _____

Level One, Lesson 1: Did You Know ...?

Did You Know ...?

- The tiniest bone in the human body is only 3 mm long and is found in your ear.

- In 1994, the population of the world was over five and a half billion people. In the year 2020, scientists estimate there will be close to eight billion people, and almost one-fifth of them will live in China.

- The average person has 120,000 hairs on his/her head; each hair grows about 3 mm per week.

- A giant redwood tree in Humboldt National Forest in California is the tallest tree on Earth. In 1991 it measured 365 feet tall, taller than a 30-story building.

- There are ten million bricks in the Empire State Building.

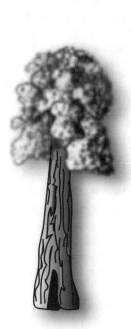

- The hornet is really just a large wasp. It is brightly striped to warn other animals that it stings. When a hornet does sting, it injects a venom that causes painful swelling.

- Of all the places on your body, your feet are the most ticklish. Nerve endings are what make you feel ticklish, and your feet have the most nerve endings.

- Sixty percent of your body is made up of water; every bone in your body contains one-fifth water. Your brain is $\frac{3}{4}$ water. You can survive weeks without food but no more than a few days without water.

- People have straight, wavy, or curly hair depending on the shape of the tiny hair follicle from which it grows. If the shape of the follicle is round, a person will have straight hair, if it is oval, a person will have wavy hair, and if it is square, a person will have tight, round curls.

- If you were to spell out the numbers ... one, two, three, etc., you would have to go to one thousand before finding the letter "a."

Level One, Lesson 1: Did You Know ...? (cont.)

- The normal body temperature is 98.6°F. A skin temperature above 104°F is very hot, and a temperature below 87.8°F is very cold. Hands feel cold when their temperature is below 68°F and go numb below 53°F. Anything above 113°F that touches your skin burns, although people have walked on hot coals at 1,472°F. Your knee can tolerate 116°F for 30 seconds.

- Half of all Americans live within 50 miles of where they were born.

- Worldwide there are over 1,500 volcanoes, 500 of them active. There are about 60 major volcanic eruptions each year around the world, including two or three huge, violent eruptions. Krakatau is a volcano in Indonesia that erupted in 1883. It produced sea waves almost 130 feet high, which drowned about 36,000 people.

- Each king in a deck of playing cards represents a great king from history. The King of Spades is King David, the King of Hearts is Charlemagne, the King of Clubs is Alexander the Great, and the King of Diamonds is Julius Caesar.

- In Scotland, a new game was invented. It was entitled Gentlemen Only Ladies Forbidden ... GOLF.

- There really is a Tasmanian devil! It is a marsupial about 20 to 30 inches long, with a foot-long bushy tail. The devil has a squarish head and a stocky body; strong teeth and jaws tear apart the meat it eats. Tasmanian devils are only found in the wild on Tasmania, an island that is part of Australia.

- Girls' brains weigh 2.5% of their body weight; boys' brains weigh 2% of their body weight.

- Rainbows can be seen at night. Bright moonlight shining through falling water creates the effect known as a "moonbow." Moonbows are much fainter than rainbows. Cumberland Falls, Kentucky, is famous for its moonbows.

- The Mona Lisa has no eyebrows.

Level One, Lesson 1: Did You Know ...? (cont.)

Reading Guide for "Did You Know ...?"

BEFORE READING

Before reading "Did You Know ...?", complete the **Before Reading** section of the Reading Guide.

A. Prereading Activity: Activating Background Knowledge

Amazing Facts

Did you know that more money is printed for Monopoly™ each day than is printed for real currency? Did you know that Coca-Cola™ was originally green? Did you know that intelligent people have more zinc and copper in their hair than other people?

Directions: There are so many amazing facts; what facts do you know? Write a few of them here and share them with others.

1. _____

  _____

2. _____

  _____

3. _____

  _____

4. _____

  _____

5. _____

  _____

Reading Engagement: Grade 7   Level One, Lesson 1: Did You Know ...?

Name: _____ Date: _____

Level One, Lesson 1: Did You Know ...? (cont.)

B. Vocabulary: Multiple Syllables

Syllables

Directions: Here are some multisyllabic vocabulary words from this reading. First tell how many syllables you hear in each word, and then divide the word into syllables. If you get stuck, try a dictionary.

Word	No. of syllables	Division of syllables
1. marsupial	_____	_____
2. gentlemen	_____	_____
3. volcanoes	_____	_____
4. temperature	_____	_____
5. follicle	_____	_____
6. depending	_____	_____
7. estimate	_____	_____
8. scientists	_____	_____
9. population	_____	_____
10. eruptions	_____	_____

C. Prereading Questions

1. What do you think this reading is going to be about?

   _____

   _____

   _____

Reading Engagement: Grade 7   Level One, Lesson 1: Did You Know ...?

Name: _____ Date: _____

Level One, Lesson 1: Did You Know ...? (cont.)

2. Read the questions in the **After Reading** section of this Reading Guide.

   a. Which question do you find the most interesting?

   _____

   _____

   b. Which answer do you think will be hardest to find?

   _____

   _____

3. What is your purpose for reading this story? Finish this sentence: I am reading to find out ...

   _____

   _____

DURING READING

1. Put a check mark in the margin next to the information that answers the questions in the **After Reading** section.

2. Circle any words you don't know when you come to them in the passage.

3. Put a question mark in the margin for anything you don't understand.

AFTER READING

1. READING THE LINES: Answer these questions by using information in the selection.

   a. What is so unusual about the Mona Lisa?

   _____

   _____

Level One, Lesson 1: Did You Know ...? (cont.)

b. Match the hair with the correct hair follicle.

straight   square

wavy   oval

curly   round

c. Who has a heavier brain, boys or girls? Why?

_____

_____

d. What makes people ticklish?

_____

_____

2. READING BETWEEN THE LINES: Answer these questions by inferring ideas in the selection.

a. In your opinion, which is the most fascinating fact?

_____

_____

b. How do you think people know there are ten million bricks in the Empire State Building?

_____

_____

c. Do you think it is true that most people live within 50 miles of where they were born? Ask five adults in your school if they live within 50 miles of where they were born. Record the results and draw a conclusion based on the results.

_____

_____

_____

Level One, Lesson 1: Did You Know ...? (cont.)

d.   Why can humans go without food much longer than they can go without water?

_____

_____

3.   READING BEYOND THE LINES: Answer these questions with your own opinions.

a.   Have you ever been stung by a hornet or a wasp? What was it like?

_____

_____

_____

b.   Draw a picture of what you think a Tasmanian devil looks like.

ASSESSMENT/REINFORCEMENT

A. Check out these websites to find new fantastic facts. Make a bulletin board out of the facts you find.

www.factmonster.com
www.timeforkids.com
www.goofball.com

Level One, Lesson 1: Did You Know ...? (cont.)

B. Crossword Puzzle: Use the reading selection and the clues below to solve the puzzle.

ACROSS

2. When the game was first invented, the word *golf* was an acronym for "Gentlemen Only Ladies _____.

7. Oval hair _____ are characteristic of people having wavy hair.

9. Tasmanian devils are only found in the wild on Tasmania, an island that is part of _____.

15. The _____ bone in your body is found in your ear.

16. There are ten million _____ in the Empire State Building.

19. Boys' _____ weigh less than girls'.

20. In a deck of cards, the King of Hearts represents _____.

DOWN

1. _____ is a volcano in Indonesia that erupted in 1883.

3. _____ are an effect created by bright moonlight shining through falling water.

4. _____ percent of your body is made up of water.

5. The King of Diamonds in a deck of cards represents _____ _____.

6. Scientists estimate that there will be close to _____ people in the year 2020.

8. In the famous painting by Leonardo da Vinci, the Mona Lisa has no _____.

10. Your feet are the most _____ places on your body.

11. You won't find an "a" in any number words when you count, until you reach the number _____ _____.

12. People have walked on _____ _____ at a temperature of 1,472°F.

13. When a hornet stings, it injects a _____ that causes painful swelling.

14. A giant _____ tree is the tallest tree on Earth and is located in Humboldt National Forest in California.

17. _____ _____ are what make you feel ticklish.

18. Scientists estimate that one-fifth of the world's _____ will live in China by the year 2020.

Level One, Lesson 2: Deep Sea Squid

Deep Sea Squid

Not long ago, scientists discovered a gigantic new type of squid in the waters of the Gulf of Mexico, and the Pacific, Atlantic, and Indian Oceans. This weird new squid has been spotted eight times—in 1988, 1992, 1998, 2000, and 2001. In May of 2001, the squid was "captured" on an underwater video from the Monterey Bay Aquarium Research Institute. The camera was trolling at a depth of more than half a mile off the coast of Oahu when it captured this ghostly white giant squid floating through the deep blue sea.

This deep sea squid has several weird features. Instead of the usual eight long arms and two modified shorter tentacles, this incredible new squid has ten equal appendages (eight called arms and two designated as tentacles), which radiate from its body like the spokes of a bicycle wheel. All ten of the appendages are bent, like an elbow, from which the rest of the tentacles hang straight down. Similar to other squid, the deep sea squid appears to have suction cups on its arms. Some scientists think these arms are used like a spider web. The squid lets its very sticky arms hang underneath its body, waiting for small crustaceans to bump into them and stick. Like a spider, the squid eats the trapped "treat." The deep sea squid also has two enormous fins that stick out from a much smaller body. These large fins flap around like elephant ears when the squid floats through the water. While it seems that the squid is floating through the water, it can actually move very quickly. The largest deep sea squid sighted was 27 feet long, larger than any other known species of squid.

The mystery squid has, so far, remained unclassified. It has never been captured nor have any of this species washed up on beaches. Scientists have not had an opportunity to examine the squid but assume their bodies are so fragile that they would get eaten by other creatures long before they reached the surface of the water.

The very weird-looking deep sea squid with its really big fins, really long arms, and really tiny body may be fairly common given the number and geography of the sightings. It does, however, make a person wonder what else lurks in the deep blue sea!

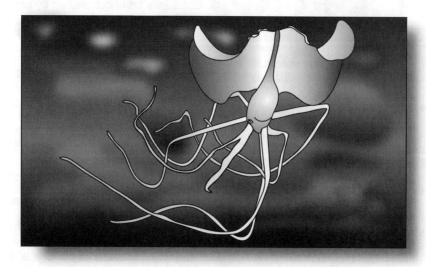

Level One, Lesson 2: Deep Sea Squid (cont.)

Reading Guide for "Deep Sea Squid"

BEFORE READING

Before reading "Deep Sea Squid," complete the **Before Reading** section of the Reading Guide.

A. Prereading Activity: Assessing Background Knowledge

True or False?

Directions: Circle "T" if you think the statement is true; circle "F" if you think the statement is false.

T   F   1.   A deep sea squid has a long, fleshy, shell-like body.

T   F   2.   A deep sea squid has two long and eight short tentacles.

T   F   3.   A deep sea squid's tentacles have suction cups for grasping objects.

T   F   4.   A deep sea squid can change color to camouflage itself.

T   F   5.   A deep sea squid has a strong jaw for biting into the hard shells of its prey.

T   F   6.   A deep sea squid has a large eye on each side of its head.

T   F   7.   A deep sea squid has a long, torpedo-like shell.

T   F   8.   Giant squids can weigh as much as 55 pounds.

T   F   9.   A deep sea squid is built much like an octopus.

T   F   10.   Some humans eat squid for food.

Level One, Lesson 2: Deep Sea Squid (cont.)

B. Vocabulary: Meaning

VOCABULARY

aquarium   trolling   Oahu   appendage   tentacles

1. One of these words is an island in the Hawaiian Islands. Which one?

   _____

2. One of these words is where captured fish and sea creatures are kept. Which one?

   _____

3. One of these words means long, flexible structures used for feeling or grasping. Which one?

   _____

4. One of these words means dragging something through the water. Which one?

   _____

5. One of these words is something attached to a larger, more important thing. Which one?

   _____

C. Prereading Questions

1. What do you think this reading is going to be about?

   _____

   _____

2. Read the questions in the **After Reading** section of this Reading Guide.

   a. Which question do you find the most interesting?

   _____

   _____

Level One, Lesson 2: Deep Sea Squid (cont.)

b. Which answer do you think will be hardest to find?

_____

_____

3. What is your purpose for reading this story? Finish this sentence: I am reading to find out ...

_____

_____

DURING READING

1. Put a check mark in the margin next to the information that answers the questions in the **After Reading** section.

2. Circle any words you don't know when you come to them in the passage.

3. Put a question mark in the margin for anything you don't understand.

AFTER READING

1. READING THE LINES: Answer these questions by using information in the selection.

    a. What does the author mean when she says the squid was "captured" on an underwater camera?

    _____

    _____

    _____

    b. Where is the island of Oahu?

    _____

    _____

Level One, Lesson 2: Deep Sea Squid (cont.)

c.   Describe the deep sea squid.

_____

_____

_____

d.   How is a squid like a spider?

_____

_____

_____

2.   READING BETWEEN THE LINES: Answer these questions by inferring ideas in the selection.

a.   Why do scientists call this squid "the mystery squid"?

_____

_____

_____

b.   What weird features does this squid have?

_____

_____

_____

c.   How is the deep sea squid like a regular squid? How is it different?

_____

_____

_____

Name: _____ Date: _____

Level One, Lesson 2: Deep Sea Squid (cont.)

3. READING BEYOND THE LINES: Answer these questions with your own opinions.

a. Are these deep sea squid more like or unlike other squid? Why do you think this?

_____

_____

_____

b. Have you ever eaten squid? Did you like it, or would you like to try it?

_____

_____

c. Look at the drawing of the deep sea squid. Label these parts on the drawing: body, arm, tentacle, fin.

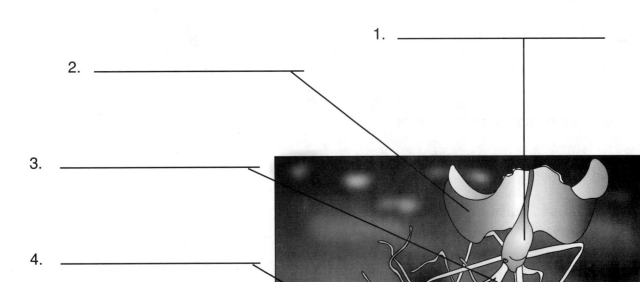

1. _____

2. _____

3. _____

4. _____

Name: _____ Date: _____

Level One, Lesson 2: Deep Sea Squid (cont.)

ASSESSMENT/REINFORCEMENT

A. Look back to the Prereading Activity about the deep sea squid. From what you now know or have learned, rewrite each statement so it is a true statement. Make a class drawing of the squid on chart paper. Label the parts of the squid, then write the ten true statements about it below your drawing. Display your knowledge of deep sea squid on a bulletin board or wall.

B. Watch for further sightings of the deep sea squid on the news or in the newspaper.

C. What are some other strange things that people claim to have seen? Research the Loch Ness Monster, mermaids, UFOs, or other mysterious sightings. Give a report to the class.

D. First Letter/Last Letter Puzzle: Use the clues below to fill in the answers in the puzzle. The last letter of the first word will be the first letter of the next word, and so on.

1. The tentacles of the deep sea squid _____ straight down.

2. Large body of water between the southern United States and Mexico (three words)

3. One of the Hawaiian Islands

4. The mystery squid has remained _____.

5. The _____ sea squid was photographed at a depth of more than half a mile.

6. One of the oceans in which the deep sea squid was seen

7. The deep sea squid has suction _____ on its arms.

8. The squid's arms may be used like a _____ web.

9. Scientists believe a dead squid may be eaten before it _____ the surface of the water.

10. The deep sea squid was _____ eight times between the years of 1998 and 2001.

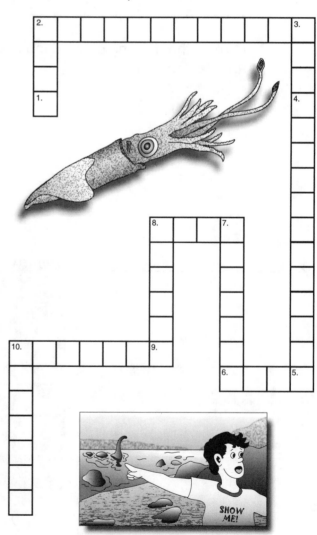

20

Name: _____   Date: _____

Level One, Lesson 3: Delicious Mistakes

Delicious Mistakes

"Intelligence is not to make no mistakes. But
quickly to see how to make them good."
— *Bertolt Brecht*

Mistakes happen in life. The successful person learns from mistakes or makes something out of the mistake. For example, Coca-Cola™ was invented by a pharmacist who was trying to make a medicinal syrup to cure headaches; instead he invented the most popular soft drink in the world. Christopher Columbus meant to sail to Asia but ended up in America. The yo-yo was invented as a weapon, not as a toy. Some of the best mistakes have resulted in something delectable.

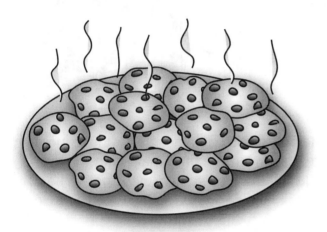

One of the most delicious mistakes was made in 1930 by Ruth Wakefield in the kitchen of her Toll House Inn. The Inn was located on the toll road between Boston and New Bedford, Massachusetts. Ruth was baking cookies and discovered she was out of baker's chocolate. She did have some semi-sweet chocolate on hand and decided to use that instead. She broke the chocolate bar into chips; Ruth thought the chips would melt and she would have chocolate cookies. To her surprise, the chips didn't melt. Instead she created the most popular cookie today: chocolate chip cookies. Nearly seven billion chocolate chip cookies are consumed per year, with Americans eating over half of these. The recipe for Ruth Wakefield's Toll House Cookies is on the back of a package of Toll House Chocolate Chips.

Another accidental mishap resulted in Brown 'n Serve rolls. Joe Gregor was a fantastic fireman and frustrated baker until these two activities collided. Joe was muttering to himself one day in 1949 about how long it took to make and bake dinner rolls and bread. He had to mix the ingredients, knead the dough, let it rise for a couple of hours, then punch and reshape the dough. Finally, he had to bake the dough for another half hour or so. Joe knew there had to be an easier way for busy people to have hot rolls for dinner, so he spent hours and hours working on a method to solve this problem—without success. Then one afternoon Joe was baking dinner rolls in his kitchen, when the fire siren began to wail. Joe was a volunteer fireman for his Florida community and had to rush to the fire. He quickly pulled his rolls out of the oven and hurried to the fire station. When he returned from the fire, he examined the cold, hard, white, half-baked rolls. Most people would have thrown them away and started again, but not Joe. He reheated his oven and finished cooking the rolls. They were scrumptious! Joe had accidentally discovered a way to make dinner rolls ahead of time, yet serve them hot and delicious at mealtime. Following his successful mistake, he experimented with oven temperatures and

Level One, Lesson 3: Delicious Mistakes (cont.)

baking times until he got them just right. Joe then revealed his method to bakers everywhere!

In 1853, Native American/African-American George Crum, a chef at the Moon Lake Resort in Saratoga Springs, New York, invented America's most popular snack food, potato chips. He invented these thin, salted, crisp chips unintentionally; he meant them as a sarcastic reply to a hostile customer. One of the items on the Moon Lake Lodge's menu was French-fried potatoes. They were prepared in the standard, thick-cut French style that was popularized in France in the 1700s and enjoyed by Thomas Jefferson who was ambassador to France. Ever since Jefferson had brought the recipe to America and served French fries to guests at Monticello, the popular dish had become serious dinner fare. At Moon Lake Lodge, one customer sent his order of French fries back to the kitchen because they were too thick for his liking. Crum cut and fried a thinner batch, but these too were rejected. This so irritated the chef (who was in a bit of a temper) that he sliced a potato paper-thin and fried the slices in very heavy oil until the "chips" were so hard they

could not be cut with a fork. Crum's attempt at contempt for his customer failed; the customer loved the potato crunchies! Other customers requested Crum's potato chips, and they were soon added to the menu of the restaurant as Saratoga Chips. The invention of the potato peeler and the potato chip bag paved the way for potato chips to soar from a small specialty item to a top-selling snack food.

Doughnut holes were a serendipitous discovery. In 1885 Hanson Gregory from Camden, Maine, was a ship captain, and it was on a fishing voyage that doughnut holes made their appearance. Captain Gregory was eating a fried cake when a huge storm suddenly arose. Gregory could not steer the ship and hold the fried cake at the same time, so he shoved the cake over one of the wheel's spokes. Without planning to, he invented the doughnut hole. After the storm, the captain ordered the ship's cook to begin making fried cakes with a hole in the middle. Since this method eliminated the sometimes soggy middle of fried cakes, Gregory's discovery became very popular. Today over $750 million worth of doughnuts are sold each year.

"Mistakes are the portals for discovery," said James Joyce, an English author. Mistakes resulted in many delicious discoveries. When intelligent people viewed their errors in new and different ways, wonderful ideas were the result.

Name: _____ Date: _____

Level One, Lesson 3: Delicious Mistakes (cont.)

Reading Guide for "Delicious Mistakes"

BEFORE READING

Before reading "Delicious Mistakes," complete the **Before Reading** section of the Reading Guide.

A. Prereading Activity: Assessing Background Knowledge

Either/Or

Directions: Answer the questions with what you know.

1. Is making a mistake a good thing or a bad thing? Why?

    _____

    _____

    _____

2. Are you usually punished or rewarded for making a mistake? How?

    _____

    _____

    _____

3. Do you like or dislike making a mistake? Why?

    _____

    _____

    _____

Level One, Lesson 3: Delicious Mistakes (cont.)

B. Vocabulary: Synonyms

Finding Synonyms

Find as many synonyms for these vocabulary words as you can.

delicious	**pharmacist**	**accidental**
_____	_____	_____
_____	_____	_____
_____	_____	_____
_____	_____	_____

C. Prereading Questions

1. What do you think this reading is going to be about?

   _____

   _____

2. Read the questions in the **After Reading** section of this Reading Guide.

   a. Which question do you find the most interesting?

      _____

      _____

   b. Which answer do you think will be hardest to find?

      _____

      _____

3. What is your purpose for reading this story? Finish this sentence: I am reading to find out...

   _____

   _____

Level One, Lesson 3: Delicious Mistakes (cont.)

DURING READING

1. Put a check mark in the margin next to the information that answers the questions in the **After Reading** section.

2. Circle any words you don't know when you come to them in the passage.

3. Put a question mark in the margin for anything you don't understand.

AFTER READING

1. READING THE LINES: Answer these questions by using information in the selection.

   a. Draw a time line showing when each of the mistakes in the reading happened.

   b. Why are chocolate chip cookies often called Toll House Cookies?

   _____

   _____

   _____

   c. The invention of the doughnut hole solved a sticky baking problem for fried cakes. What was the problem?

   _____

   _____

   _____

   d. Where was fireman Joe Gregor from?

   _____

Name: _____ Date: _____

Level One, Lesson 3: Delicious Mistakes (cont.)

2. READING BETWEEN THE LINES: Answer these questions by inferring ideas in the selection.

   a.   What is the main idea of this reading?

   _____

   _____

   _____

   _____

   b.   How was the invention of potato chips a mistake?

   _____

   _____

   _____

   c.   Compare what a successful person does with a mistake to what an unsuccessful person does.

   _____

   _____

   _____

   d.   How did French fries become one of America's favorite foods?

   _____

   _____

   _____

Level One, Lesson 3: Delicious Mistakes (cont.)

3. READING BEYOND THE LINES: Answer these questions with your own opinions.

   a. Have you ever made bread from scratch? Describe the process. Describe the results.

   _____

   _____

   _____

   _____

   b. Do you know of any delicious mistakes not mentioned here?

   _____

   _____

   _____

   c. Draw a picture of the ship's wheel with the fried cake on one of the spokes of the wheel.

ASSESSMENT/REINFORCEMENT

A. Here is a list of other delicious mistakes. Choose one and research the story of its invention.

   Ice Cream Cone   Fudge   Popsicles™
                  Sandwiches   Coca-Cola™

Level One, Lesson 3: Delicious Mistakes (cont.)

B. Some of the following brand names/logos were actual people or based on actual people, while others were an artist's drawing and don't represent a real person. Using the Internet or other reference sources, research to find out which was which. Circle "yes" if the name represents a real person or "no" if the name doesn't represent a real person. Then draw a line to the corresponding product.

Yes No	1.	Clarence Birdseye	A. Cookbooks
Yes No	2.	Russell Stover	B. Bananas
Yes No	3.	Mr. Peanut	C. Ice cream
Yes No	4.	Howard Johnson	D. Flour/Baking
Yes No	5.	Miss Chiquita	E. Pancakes
Yes No	6.	Uncle Ben	F. Peanuts
Yes No	7.	Colonel Sanders	G. Cereal
Yes No	8.	Fannie Farmer	H. Fried chicken
Yes No	9.	Little Debbie	I. Restaurants/Hotels
Yes No	10.	Ben & Jerry	J. Baby food
Yes No	11.	Aunt Jemima	K. Candy
Yes No	12.	Gerber Baby	L. Rice
Yes No	13.	Betty Crocker	M. Frozen vegetables
Yes No	14.	Tony the Tiger	N. Snack cakes

Name: _____ Date: _____

Level Two, Lesson 1: Totally Absurd Inventions ... for Pets

Totally Absurd Inventions ... for Pets

Throughout history, people have been inventing stuff. Sometimes inventors create totally new stuff that improves our standard of living significantly. Sometimes inventors merely improve upon existing inventions to make life easier or more fun. Sometimes inventions are just totally goofy. Read about these wacky pet inventions; maybe you will get an idea for a "totally absurd invention" for your pet!

Doggie Umbrella

If your dog won't go out in the rain to do his duty, then this invention is for you. The Doggie Umbrella consists of an umbrella frame mounted to a harness and covered with a fully draped clear plastic, complete with front air holes so the dog can breathe. The front air holes also keep the plastic from fogging up. What do you suppose would happen to the umbrella if the dog suddenly decided to tear after a rabbit or squirrel? Ouch!

Pet Toilet

An elegant ramp leads to the pet commode, which rests comfortably on top of a conventional toilet. A sensing device detects movement by the pet; as the pet departs, the commode automatically flushes water from the perforated tube around the perimeter of the device. When the trap door reopens, the "waste" is gone. Voilá!

Doggie Luggage

Going on a trip? Not wanting to "store" your pet in the cargo area? Can't walk your dog on a leash through the airport? This invention is for you. Doggie Luggage is not luggage for dogs; instead, the dog is the luggage. This luggage looks like an ordinary cloth suitcase with one side removed (for the dog's head) and four bottom holes for the dog's legs. You and Poochie will move swiftly through airports with Doggie Luggage. If you buy now, as an extra bonus, you will receive the convenient shoulder strap: no more tired hands, just sling Poochie over your shoulder and go!

Level Two, Lesson 1: Totally Absurd Inventions...for Pets (cont.)

Pet Shower

Got a dirty dog or a cunning cat? Hate having to bathe your pet? Tired of chasing your pet, holding your pet, getting wet from your pet, or being bitten or scratched by your pet during bath time? The Pet Shower takes the hassle out of cleaning your pet! This doghouse-shaped vinyl enclosure has a hole for the dog's head to protrude. An attached sprinkler-like system showers your pet with water from the attached hose connection. Now you can shower your pet without showering yourself! Cool!

Pet Petter

No time to pet your animal? Scratching, stroking, and petting can be time-consuming; with a Pet Petter, you can virtually eliminate this chore. When your pet gets near the petter, an electric eye spots the movement and sends a signal to the electronic motors to begin swinging the petting arm. A human-like hand is attached to the swinging arm and scratches your pet in a repetitive motion. The inventor of the Pet Petter suggests that it can also be used on human babies. Yikes!

Dog Bell

The Dog Bell is a convenience every pet owner should have, especially if you hate to go out with your dog in the winter or in the rain. With the Dog Bell, you let the dog out, and he rings the bell to get back in. This unique product is a small (12″ x 8″) scratch pad mounted next to the back door. The pad is attached to an electrical current. When the dog wants back in, he scratches the pad, which rings the bell. Electricity? In the rain? Yee-oww!

Animal Ear Protectors

Animal Ear Protectors are designed to do much the same as a girl's headband—to keep hair out of the face. The Protectors keep the dog's ears away from its head and out of its face when it eats. Tube-like protectors contain and protect each of the dog's ears. Like a girl, a dog can sport pigtails! Sha-zamm!

Name: _____ Date: _____

Level Two, Lesson 1: Totally Absurd Inventions...for Pets (cont.)

Reading Guide for "Totally Absurd Inventions ... for Pets"

BEFORE READING

Before reading "Totally Absurd Inventions ... for Pets," complete the **Before Reading** section of the Reading Guide.

A. Prereading Activity: Assessing Background Knowledge

Inventors and Their Inventions

Directions: Match the inventors in the first column to their inventions in the second column.

_____　1.　Alexander Graham Bell　　　　a.　airplane

_____　2.　Wright Brothers　　　　　　　b.　windshield wipers

_____　3.　William Kellogg　　　　　　　c.　telephone

_____　4.　Mary Anderson　　　　　　　d.　Black History Month

_____　5.　Carter Woodson　　　　　　　e.　cornflakes

B. Vocabulary: Defining Meanings

Definitions

Directions: Define each of these words in your own words or from a dictionary.

1.　significantly _____

2.　virtually _____

3.　eliminate _____

4.　repetitive _____

5.　unique _____

6.　cunning _____

Name: _____ Date: _____

Level Two, Lesson 1: Totally Absurd Inventions...for Pets (cont.)

7. perforated _____

8. elegant _____

9. conventional _____

10. cargo _____

C. Prereading Questions

1. What do you think this reading is going to be about?

_____

_____

2. Read the questions in the **After Reading** section of this Reading Guide.

   a. Which question do you find the most interesting?

   _____

   _____

   b. Which answer do you think will be hardest to find?

   _____

   _____

3. What is your purpose for reading this story? Finish this sentence: I am reading to find out ...

_____

_____

Level Two, Lesson 1: Totally Absurd Inventions...for Pets (cont.)

DURING READING

1. Put a check mark in the margin next to the information that answers the questions in the **After Reading** section.

2. Circle any words you don't know when you come to them in the passage.

3. Put a question mark in the margin for anything you don't understand.

AFTER READING

1. READING THE LINES: Answer these questions by using information in the selection.

   a. What word could be substituted for the word *stuff* in sentences 1 and 2?

   _____

   b. The first paragraph uses three different adjectives to describe the inventions in this reading. What are they?

      1. Totally _____ inventions ...

      2. Totally _____ inventions ....

      3. Totally _____ inventions ....

   c. Which of the inventions offers a bonus for buying now?

   _____

   _____

   d. What reason does the author give for buying a Pet Petter?

   _____

   _____

Level Two, Lesson 1: Totally Absurd Inventions...for Pets (cont.)

2. READING BETWEEN THE LINES: Answer these questions by inferring ideas in the selection.

    a.   All but one of the descriptive paragraphs contains a one-word interjection. Which one does not?

_____

    b.   Answer this question posed at the end of the description about the Doggie Umbrella: What do you suppose would happen to the umbrella if the dog suddenly decided to tear after a rabbit or a squirrel?

_____

_____

_____

    c.   What does "tear after" mean in the sentence above?

_____

_____

    d.   In your mind, what does the Pet Shower look like? Draw a picture of it in the box below.

Name: _____ Date: _____

Level Two, Lesson 1: Totally Absurd Inventions...for Pets (cont.)

3. READING BEYOND THE LINES: Answer these questions with your own opinions.

a. What is an interjection? What interjection would work in the paragraph that is without one? (See #2a above.)

_____

_____

_____

b. What is your favorite wacky pet invention? Why is it your favorite?

_____

_____

_____

c. What might be the disadvantages of using the Pet Petter on human babies?

_____

_____

_____

_____

ASSESSMENT/REINFORCEMENT

A. You can be an inventor too! Think of an idea for a "totally absurd invention" for a pet. On your own paper, draw a diagram of it; label the separate parts of the diagram; and write a descriptive paragraph that explains what your invention is, for what it is intended, and who might use it.

B. In concert with others, make a bulletin board of your ideas under the banner: Totally Absurd Inventions!

Name: _____ Date: _____

Level Two, Lesson 2: Go for Broke!

"Go for Broke!"

Japanese-American soldiers during World War II had to fight two battles: one against the Nazis, and the other against discrimination. When the Japanese attacked Pearl Harbor on December 7, 1941, Japanese-Americans were viewed as the enemy, despite the fact that they were American citizens. The prevailing view was that no Japanese could be trusted.

When the United States entered World War II in 1941, there were 5,000 Japanese-Americans in the armed forces. Most of them were removed from their combat units, and college soldiers were removed from their ROTC units. The Nisei—second generation Japanese-Americans—were classified as 4-C, "enemy aliens," despite the fact they were American citizens; they were not allowed to enlist in the U.S. military.

Japanese-Americans on the west coast were relocated and incarcerated in internment camps located in barren regions of California and Montana. Japanese-Americans in Hawaii escaped the "enemy alien roundup" because they were an important part of the local economy. The island simply couldn't function without them.

In 1943, President Roosevelt and the War Department decided to allow Japanese-Americans to volunteer for an all-Japanese-American regiment to fight for their country in World War II. Approximately 1,500 men from the mainland and 3,000 Nisei from Hawaii volunteered. Most believed it was the only way Japanese-Americans would be recognized as loyal Americans. The Nisei soldiers were bright-eyed, well-dressed, and well-mannered. The soldiers looked sharp despite their small stature—the average height was 5´3´´, average weight, 125 pounds.

The Nisei soldiers were organized into the 442nd Regiment and fought in eight major campaigns in Italy, France, and Germany, including the battles at Belmont, Bruyeres, and Biffontaine. They made two beachhead assaults and captured a submarine. In France, they liberated Bruyeres and rescued the "Lost Battalion." The Alamo Regiment (so named because of their San Antonio origin) had been cut off and surrounded by Germans for six days in the fall of 1944 without food and water in the heavy forests of the Vosges Mountains. The 442nd was sent into the rugged terrain to rescue the surrounded soldiers. In this bloody confrontation, the 442nd unit lost more than 800 men.

Reading Engagement: Grade 7　　　　　　　　　　　Level Two, Lesson 2: Go for Broke!

Name: _____　Date: _____

Level Two, Lesson 2: Go for Broke! (cont.)

Nearly 2,000 Nisei soldiers from the 442nd served in military intelligence, using their linguistic skills to penetrate enemy lines, break secret codes, translate documents, and perform a variety of other tasks. Called Merle's Marauders, the Nisei troops parachuted into the jungles of Burma. There they not only captured Japanese documents and translated them, they endured unbelievable casualties; of the 2,000 soldiers, only about 200 survived.

The 442nd Field Artillery Battalion was among the first Allied units to liberate prisoners from Dachau. The survivors of Dachau were totally perplexed by the Japanese soldiers in American uniforms. They didn't know which salute to give—the "Heil, Hitler" salute or the U.S. military salute. Days later, the soldiers helped save more than 5,000 Jewish prisoners from the Dachau sub-camps who had been on a forced march toward the Bavarian Alps. Nisei soldiers gave the liberated people food, medicine, and bedding. After the unit was ordered to move on, some Nisei soldiers stayed and set up temporary soup kitchens for the survivors.

Because the 442nd was often sent into some of the most dangerous situations of the war, they adopted the motto, "Go for Broke!" In less than two years of combat, the 442nd Regimental Combat Team earned more than 18,143 decorations for bravery. These individual medals included one Medal of Honor, 53 Distinguished Service Crosses, 588 Silver Stars, 5,200 Bronze Star Medals, 9,486 Purple Hearts, and eight Presidential Unit Citations (the nation's top award for combat units).

Due to their outstanding bravery and the heavy combat duty they faced, the 442nd RCT became the most decorated unit in U.S. military history for its size and length of service. Known as the "Purple Heart Battalion," the Nisei Regimental Combat Team made a major contribution to the freedom we enjoy as Americans.

In all, more than 15 million Americans served in the military during World War II, and over 400,000 lost their lives.

Level Two, Lesson 2: Go for Broke! (cont.)

Reading Guide for "Go for Broke!"

BEFORE READING

Before reading "Go for Broke!", complete the **Before Reading** section of the Reading Guide.

A. Prereading Activity: Building Background Knowledge

Japanese in America in World War II

Directions: Read the paragraph, and then answer the questions.

The United States declared war on Japan immediately following Japan's devastating attack on Pearl Harbor, December 7, 1941. At the time, there were about 300,000 Japanese and Japanese-Americans living in the United States. Most of the Japanese who immigrated to the U.S. settled in California and Hawaii. The U.S. War Department believed that Japanese-Americans posed a threat of sabotage and that no person of Japanese descent could be trusted. Therefore, the War Relocation Authority began to round up persons considered "risky" and persons living in any "military zone." About 110,000 Japanese-Americans were crowded into American concentration camps, despite the fact that many of these "detainees" were American citizens and that over half the 110,000 were children. Those relocated by government order suffered both material losses in property and wages, not to mention the restrictions on their religious, political, and civic freedoms.

1. Do you think the government was right to "detain" Japanese-American citizens during World War II?

   _____

   _____

   _____

2. The U.S. was also at war with Germany and Italy. Why were no German-Americans or Italian-Americans "detained"?

   _____

   _____

   _____

   _____

Name: _____ Date: _____

Level Two, Lesson 2: Go for Broke! (cont.)

B. Vocabulary: Word Meaning

"Go for Broke!" Vocabulary

Directions: Read over the vocabulary words from this selection. Be sure you can pronounce the words and know their meanings. Then use each word correctly in a sentence.

alien	campaigns	casualties
discrimination	incarcerated	internment
linguistic	perplexed	relocate
stature		

1. _____

_____

2. _____

_____

3. _____

_____

4. _____

_____

5. _____

_____

6. _____

_____

7. _____

_____

8. _____

_____

9. _____

_____

10. _____

_____

Reading Engagement: Grade 7   Level Two, Lesson 2: Go for Broke!

Name: _____ Date: _____

Level Two, Lesson 2: Go for Broke! (cont.)

C. Prereading Questions

1. What do you think this reading is going to be about?

   _____

   _____

2. Read the questions in the **After Reading** section of this Reading Guide.

   a. Which question do you find the most interesting?

   _____

   _____

   b. Which answer do you think will be hardest to find?

   _____

   _____

3. What is your purpose for reading this story? Finish this sentence: I am reading to find out ...

   _____

   _____

DURING READING

1. Put a check mark in the margin next to the information that answers the questions in the **After Reading** section.

2. Circle any words you don't know when you come to them in the passage.

3. Put a question mark in the margin for anything you don't understand.

Reading Engagement: Grade 7   Level Two, Lesson 2: Go for Broke!

Name: _____ Date: _____

Level Two, Lesson 2: Go for Broke! (cont.)

AFTER READING

1. READING THE LINES: Answer these questions by using information in the selection.

   a. What is a Nisei?

   _____

   _____

   b. What was the "Lost Battalion"?

   _____

   _____

   c. What was the "enemy alien round-up"?

   _____

   _____

   _____

   d. Why were the Japanese-American soldiers called the "Purple Heart Brigade"?

   _____

   _____

2. READING BETWEEN THE LINES: Answer these questions by inferring ideas in the selection.

   a. Explain in your own words what is meant by the first sentence in this reading.

   _____

   _____

   _____

Name: _____ Date: _____

Level Two, Lesson 2: Go for Broke! (cont.)

b. Were the rights of the Japanese-Americans violated during World War II? Why or why not? If so, how?

_____

_____

_____

c. Why did so many Japanese-American men volunteer to fight during World War II?

_____

_____

_____

d. How did Nisei soldiers differ from other American soldiers?

_____

_____

3. READING BEYOND THE LINES: Answer these questions with your own opinions.

a. Can you name another group of soldiers who faced similar racial discrimination in the American armed forces? Who were they, and what was their story?

_____

_____

_____

b. Not many people know the history of the 442nd RCT. What ideas do you have for getting this story out to the general public?

_____

_____

_____

Name: _____ Date: _____

Level Two, Lesson 2: Go for Broke! (cont.)

c. Do you think the Nisei soldiers feel appreciated for what they did during World War II? Why or why not?

_____

_____

_____

_____

d. In all, approximately how many Americans lost their lives in World War II?

_____

ASSESSMENT/REINFORCEMENT

Directions: The paragraphs below describe the injustices against the Japanese-Americans during World War II. Unscramble each of the words to complete the paragraphs.

There was CJREUPDIE _____ against Japanese-Americans even before the attack on APLER RHAOBR _____; however, after the attack, the prejudice greatly increased. Although the Japanese-Americans were loyal U.S. SCTINIZE _____, many people feared they would side with PNJAA _____. As a result, the basic NUHMA STIGRH _____ _____ of the Japanese-Americans were abused. Their homes were RHSECEDA _____ for cameras, radios, and weapons in the fear they would be used against the United States. They were assigned numbers and had to register with the EGETOVRNMN _____. In 1942, President VORLOSEET _____ ordered the evacuation of Japanese-Americans from the west coast. They had to leave their homes to go to one of ten TERNINTEMN _____ camps in California, Colorado, Utah, Arkansas, and other states.

The government wanted everyone to believe that the Japanese-Americans accepted the OEARLOCTIN _____ as a wartime necessity. Although they did not want to leave their homes, the Japanese-Americans cooperated with the government to

Level Two, Lesson 2: Go for Broke! (cont.)

show their YLOLYAT _____ to their country.

The barracks at the internment camps were crowded and offered little YVPIACR _____. Each family had a small space in which to live, with a single light bulb providing the only light. They slept on cots. The camps were surrounded by RABEDB RWIE _____ _____ and AGDURS _____.

After about a year, the Japanese-Americans were allowed to go home. Unfortunately, many of their homes and farms had been DTDESRYOE _____; their personal PEPOYRRT _____ and possessions were gone. They had to begin again, looking for OJSB _____ and GIUHOSN _____. No Japanese-Americans were ever convicted or accused of GYISPN _____ or NTARESO _____ during World War II. In fact, 33,000 Japanese-Americans served in the MADRE ERFOCS _____ _____; two of the most TEODECRAD _____ units in the war were Japanese-American.

In 1980, a government commission reported that the internment of Japanese-Americans was due to "race prejudice, war hysteria, and a EILFUAR _____ of political leadership." The government apologized, and the surviving Japanese-Americans were each given a AYNPMET _____ of $20,000.

Level Two, Lesson 3: Bill of Rights, Part I

Bill of Rights, Part I

When the United States Constitution was created, a number of statesmen were worried that it put too much power into the hands of the federal government. Some states wouldn't ratify the Constitution until a "bill of rights" was drafted to accompany it; other states ratified the Constitution with the provision that a "bill of rights" be amended to it.

George Mason, a delegate of the Constitutional Convention, expressed great concern that assurances of individual liberties had not been incorporated into the Constitution. Because of this concern, he refused to sign the document and left the Constitutional Convention bitterly disappointed. However, George Mason's views were heard, and when James Madison drafted the amendments to the Constitution that were to become the Bill of Rights, he drew heavily upon Mason's ideas put forth in the Virginia Declaration of Rights. Other influences were the English Bill of Rights (1689), the Magna Carta (1215), the Articles of Confederation (1781), and the Declaration of Independence (1776).

Finally, on December 15, 1791, three years after the Constitution was ratified, the new United States of America adopted the Bill of Rights. The first paragraph in the document described the purpose of the Bill of Rights: *"The Conventions of a number of States having, at the time of adopting the Constitution, expressed a desire, in order to prevent misconstruction or abuse of its powers, that further declaratory and restrictive clauses should be added, and as extending the ground of public confidence in the Government will best insure the beneficent ends of its institution ..."* (The Bill of Rights).

The first ten amendments to the U.S. Constitution, known as the Bill of Rights, confirm the fundamental rights of its citizens. The Bill of Rights establishes basic American civil liberties that the federal government cannot violate. Originally, the Bill of Rights applied only to the federal government, but with the ratification of the 14th amendment, most of the provisions also apply to the states.

First Amendment

The First Amendment guarantees freedom of speech, freedom of the press, freedom of religion, and freedom of association and assembly. Also protected are the rights of citizens not to be forced to support someone else's religion. The First Amendment also provides for the right to demand a change in governmental policies.

Second Amendment

The Second Amendment states that *"A well regulated militia, being necessary to the security of a free state, the right of the people to keep and bear arms, shall not be infringed."*

Name: _____ Date: _____

Level Two, Lesson 3: Bill of Rights, Part I (cont.)

Third Amendment

The Third Amendment forbids the federal government from assigning soldiers to live in private residences during peacetime without the resident's permission. During the American Revolution, American colonists were forced to feed and house British soldiers. Because the colonists really resented this practice, they banned it with this amendment. The Third Amendment has never been the subject of interpretation by the courts. This amendment has been irrelevant since it was ratified because the American government has never used this practice in housing its soldiers.

Fourth Amendment

The Fourth Amendment guards against unreasonable search and seizure; the police do not have the right to search people's homes or offices, nor can they seize people's property without reasonable grounds. The Fourth Amendment guarantees that no one—no matter how dangerous—may be thrown in jail without protection of his basic rights. Americans have the right to go to their homes and be left alone by the government; Americans have the right to privacy and personal security; and Americans have the right to protection of their privacy and possessions. This amendment guarantees that no one can be arrested without a warrant and prohibits the police from using deadly force to arrest someone unless the person poses a threat of death or serious injury to the policeman or others.

The Fifth Amendment

The Fifth Amendment provides five important protections from arbitrary government actions. First, no one can be prosecuted for a federal crime without first being indicted by a grand jury. Second, a suspect cannot be tried twice for the same crime. Third, a person cannot be forced to testify against himself. Fourth, a person has the right to due process (being treated fairly). Fifth, the government does not have the right to deprive anyone of his private property unless it is necessary for a public purpose and unless the government pays a fair price for it.

There are a number of important "terms" guaranteed by the Fifth Amendment: due process, double jeopardy, grand jury, self-incrimination, and eminent domain. The purpose of a grand jury is to limit the power of the federal government to prosecute citizens, and in prosecuting cannot force a person to incriminate himself. Interestingly, this does not apply to service personnel on active duty; they are subject to a court martial. Double jeopardy prevents either state or federal authorities from bringing the same person to trial more than once for the same offense after he has been acquitted by a jury. Eminent domain is the power of the government to acquire private property for public use. Property taken must be used in such a manner that benefits the public, and the owner must be paid a fair price for the property. Due process compels the government to play fair in the laws that it creates and in depriving any person of life, liberty, or property. Due process reinforces the American value that the end does not justify the means.

Level Two, Lesson 3: Bill of Rights, Part I (cont.)

Reading Guide for "Bill of Rights, Part I"

BEFORE READING

Before reading "Bill of Rights, Part 1," complete the **Before Reading** section of the Reading Guide.

A. Prereading Activity: Assessing Background Knowledge

What Do You Think?

Directions: Answer the questions about each scenario below with what you know about the Bill of Rights.

1. A criminal robs a bank. This is a crime under both state and federal law. He is tried in state court and found guilty. Can he now be tried in federal court for this same crime? Why or why not?

   _____

   _____

   _____

2. Mr. and Mrs. Smith refuse medical treatment for their two-year-old daughter who is very ill, because such treatment would violate their religious beliefs. Can the government force them to get treatment for their daughter? Why or why not?

   _____

   _____

   _____

3. The Ku Klux Klan wants to erect a cross in a public square near the state capitol during the Christmas season. Can the government legally stop them from doing this? Why or why not?

   _____

   _____

   _____

Level Two, Lesson 3: Bill of Rights, Part I (cont.)

B. Vocabulary: Alphabetical Order/Synonyms

Vocabulary Word Bank

ratify	amend	irrelevant	prosecute	indicted
incriminate	arbitrary	jeopardy	acquit	eminent

Directions: Arrange the vocabulary words in alphabetical order, and then write a synonym for each word.

Alphabetical Order   **Synonym**

1. _____   _____

2. _____   _____

3. _____   _____

4. _____   _____

5. _____   _____

6. _____   _____

7. _____   _____

8. _____   _____

9. _____   _____

10. _____   _____

C. Prereading Questions

1. What do you think this reading is going to be about?

   _____

   _____

2. Read the questions in the **After Reading** section of this Reading Guide.

   a.   Which question do you find the most interesting?

   _____

   _____

Name: _____ Date: _____

Level Two, Lesson 3: Bill of Rights, Part I (cont.)

b.   Which answer do you think will be hardest to find?

_____

_____

3.   What is your purpose for reading this story? Finish this sentence: I am reading to find out ...

_____

_____

DURING READING

1.   Put a check mark in the margin next to the information that answers the questions in the **After Reading** section.

2.   Circle any words you don't know when you come to them in the passage.

3.   Put a question mark in the margin for anything you don't understand.

AFTER READING

1.   READING THE LINES: Answer these questions by using information in the selection.

a.   Why did some citizens believe that a Bill of Rights was a necessary part of the Constitution?

_____

_____

_____

b.   Who was George Mason, and what did he have to do with the Bill of Rights?

_____

_____

_____

Level Two, Lesson 3: Bill of Rights, Part I (cont.)

c. What other documents influenced the author of the Bill of Rights?

_____

_____

_____

d. Which amendment has been irrelevant since it was written? Why?

_____

_____

_____

e. Identify the Amendment about which each of these terms applies:

1. freedom of speech   _____

2. due process   _____

3. freedom of religion   _____

4. search and seizure   _____

5. eminent domain   _____

6. right to bear arms   _____

2. READING BETWEEN THE LINES: Answer these questions by inferring ideas in the selection.

a. Why is the Bill of Rights so important to Americans?

_____

_____

_____

Name: _____ Date: _____

 # Level Two, Lesson 3: Bill of Rights, Part I (cont.)

b.   What is double jeopardy? Why is this important?

_____

_____

_____

_____

c.   When people "plead the Fifth" in a jury trial, what are they saying, and what right are they invoking?

_____

_____

_____

3.   READING BEYOND THE LINES: Answer these questions with your own opinions.

a.   Of the rights discussed so far, which right do you think is most important? Why?

_____

_____

_____

_____

b.   Do you think the government should have the right to take your property for public use even if they have to pay you for it? Why or why not?

_____

_____

_____

Name: _____ Date: _____

Level Two, Lesson 3: Bill of Rights, Part I (cont.)

ASSESSMENT/REINFORCEMENT

A. Look in local, state, and national newspapers for stories that illustrate the rights protected in the Bill of Rights. Assemble a display or notebook containing at least ten examples of instances where citizens' rights are involved. Focus on those rights outlined in the first five amendments to the Constitution: freedom of religion, speech, press, assembly, and petition; right to bear arms; protection from unreasonable searches and seizures; indictment by a grand jury; no double jeopardy; not being a witness against oneself; the right to due process of law; and the power of eminent domain.

B. True/False: If the statement is true, circle the "T." If the statement is false, circle the "F."

T   F   1. All the states refused to ratify the Constitution until a "bill of rights" was added to it.

T   F   2. Many of George Mason's ideas from the Virginia Declaration of Rights were used in the Bill of Rights.

T   F   3. Thomas Jefferson wrote the Bill of Rights.

T   F   4. The Bill of Rights only applies to the federal government.

T   F   5. The government can take private property for public use through the power of eminent domain.

T   F   6. The police cannot search your home unless they have a search warrant.

T   F   7. The First Amendment guarantees everyone the right to say whatever they want.

T   F   8. Double jeopardy means that fines may be doubled for federal crimes.

T   F   9. The Third Amendment was included in the Bill of Rights because Americans resented the British quartering soldiers in private homes.

T   F   10. Under due process of the law, the only person not subject to the laws of the land is the President of the United States.

Name: _____ Date: _____

Level Two, Lesson 4: Bill of Rights, Part II

Bill of Rights, Part II

The first ten amendments to the U.S. Constitution have been pivotal to both the legal and political development of America. These amendments, also known as the Bill of Rights, accomplish three important purposes. First, they reinforce the American value that people have rights with which no government may interfere. Second, they provide a way to secure these rights through the court system. Third, they protect democracy by disallowing criminal prosecutions against people who criticize the government or those who have unpopular beliefs.

The First Amendment guarantees freedom of religion, speech, press, and freedom to assemble in groups. Other amendments guarantee the collective right to keep and bear arms, to freedom from unlawful searches and seizures, the right to due process of law, to a speedy and public trial, to trial by jury, and to protection from cruel and unusual punishment. The first ten amendments to the Constitution define the scope of individual freedom and serve to make our political system more democratic.

Sixth Amendment

The Sixth Amendment guarantees that people who are accused of crimes are innocent until proven guilty. In all criminal proceedings, the government has the burden of proving the accused is guilty; the accused does not have the burden of proving he is innocent. This amendment specifies procedural rights granted to all persons charged with a federal crime. The accused has the right to a speedy trial; the government may not purposefully and deliberately jail a person awaiting trial for an unnecessarily long time. The accused has the right to a public trial; this amendment assures that secret inquisitions are wrong. Justice must be carried out under the eyes of its citizens. A person accused of a crime has the right to face his accuser. Additional rights guaranteed by the Sixth Amendment are the right to an attorney, the right to know why he is being charged, and the right to be tried where the crime was committed.

Seventh Amendment

The Seventh Amendment, one of the few amendments that does not apply to the states, guarantees the right to a jury in some types of federal civil (noncriminal) trials. This amendment gives a person a right to a jury trial for monetary damages in federal court. Civil lawsuits are prosecuted in federal courts where money is involved.

Name: _____ Date: _____

Level Two, Lesson 4: Bill of Rights, Part II (cont.)

Eighth Amendment

The Eighth Amendment prohibits the use of cruel or unusual punishment. Punishment that is inhumane, barbaric, or degrading is prohibited by the Eighth Amendment. The amendment guarantees that the conditions in prisons, mental hospitals, and prisoner-of-war camps must be humane. The death penalty is not considered cruel or unusual punishment, but executions must be humane. Prisoners cannot be tortured to death, but may be electrocuted, gassed, shot by a firing squad, or given a lethal injection. Excessive bail or fines are also prohibited by the Eighth Amendment.

Ninth Amendment

The Ninth Amendment reiterates that all human beings have certain rights with which they are "endowed by their creator," that they possess simply because they are human beings. These rights are the right to life, liberty, and the pursuit of happiness. The Ninth Amendment also protects fundamental rights that are not included in the Constitution, such as the right to engage in political activity and the right of personal privacy. The Ninth Amendment protects the rights of the minority from the will of the majority.

Tenth Amendment

The Tenth Amendment is another one of those amendments added to reduce the fears that the new national government might someday seek to exceed its proper power. The Tenth Amendment restates the relationships already established between the states and the federal government. If a particular power is not assigned to the federal government by the Constitution, then the power falls to the states. This amendment guarantees that people are free to act, without permission of the federal government, in areas outside the scope of the federal government's powers.

The Bill of Rights, the first ten amendments to the Constitution of the United States, establishes basic American civil liberties that the federal government cannot violate. The Bill of Rights defines the scope of individual freedom and insures a democratic government.

Level Two, Lesson 4: Bill of Rights, Part II (cont.)

Reading Guide for "Bill of Rights, Part II"

BEFORE READING

Before reading "Bill of Rights, Part II," complete the **Before Reading** section of the Reading Guide.

A. Prereading Activity: What Do You Think?

Directions: Answer each question about which of Joe's rights is being violated in each scenario below and list the corresponding amendments.

1. Police go into Joe Martin's house, arrest him, and take him to the police station for interrogation. They have no warrant and don't tell him why he's being arrested. Which of his rights is being violated?

   _____

   _____

   _____

2. When the police take Joe to the police station, they interrogate him without an attorney present. He is left in jail for several weeks. Which of his rights is being violated?

   _____

   _____

   _____

3. To get out of jail, he is told that bail is set at $1,000,000 for the theft of several CDs. Which of his rights is being violated?

   _____

   _____

   _____

4. After a trial in which Joe is forced to testify against himself, he is found guilty of stealing several CDs and is fined $250,000. Which of his rights is being violated?

   _____

   _____

   _____

Level Two, Lesson 4: Bill of Rights, Part II (cont.)

B.   Vocabulary: Alphabetical Order/Synonyms

Vocabulary Word Bank

pivotal	guarantee	inquisitions	accuser	monetary
humane	electrocute	lethal	reiterates	scope

Directions: Arrange the vocabulary words in alphabetical order, and then write a synonym for each word.

Alphabetical Order   **Synonym**

1. _____   _____

2. _____   _____

3. _____   _____

4. _____   _____

5. _____   _____

6. _____   _____

7. _____   _____

8. _____   _____

9. _____   _____

10. _____   _____

C. Prereading Questions

1.   What do you think this reading is going to be about?

   _____

   _____

2.   Read the questions in the **After Reading** section of this Reading Guide.

   a.   Which question do you find the most interesting?

   _____

   _____

Level Two, Lesson 4: Bill of Rights, Part II (cont.)

b.   Which answer do you think will be hardest to find?

_____

_____

3.   What is your purpose for reading this story? Finish this sentence: I am reading to find out ...

_____

_____

DURING READING

1.   Put a check mark in the margin next to the information that answers the questions in the
     After Reading section.

2.   Circle any words you don't know when you come to them in the passage.

3.   Put a question mark in the margin for anything you don't understand.

AFTER READING

1.   READING THE LINES: Answer these questions by using information in the selection.

a.   What three important purposes does the Bill of Rights accomplish?

_____

_____

_____

_____

_____

Level Two, Lesson 4: Bill of Rights, Part II (cont.)

2. **READING BETWEEN THE LINES:** Answer these questions by inferring ideas in the selection.

a. What rights does an accused person have?

_____

_____

_____

_____

b. What does it mean that executions must be humane?

_____

_____

_____

c. Why was the Tenth Amendment included in the Bill of Rights?

_____

_____

_____

3. **READING BEYOND THE LINES:** Answer these questions with your own opinions.

a. Which right do you think is most important? Why?

_____

_____

_____

Level Two, Lesson 4: Bill of Rights, Part II (cont.)

b. Do you think the death penalty is cruel or unusual punishment? Why or why not?

_____

_____

_____

_____

c. If you could add an amendment, what would you add?

_____

_____

_____

ASSESSMENT/REINFORCEMENT

A. You have been asked by your principal to explain to some new immigrant students what the Bill of Rights is and why it is important to Americans. Put together a presentation (any type: editorial, letter, speech, etc.) that includes at least one visual display. Give your presentation.

B. Using the list of rights, put each one under the number of the corresponding Amendment on the next page.

- Rights to life, liberty, and the pursuit of happiness
- Right to a jury trial for monetary damages in federal court
- Right to privacy and personal security
- Cannot be jailed without protection of basic rights
- Cannot be arrested without a warrant
- Freedom of association and assembly
- Prohibits use of cruel or unusual punishment
- Protection against being forced to house soldiers
- Guards against unreasonable search and seizure
- Right to an attorney
- Right to a speedy and impartial trial
- Prevents excessive bail being charged
- Powers not assigned to the federal government are held by the states or the people

- Freedom of speech
- Right to bear arms
- Due process of law
- Double jeopardy
- Freedom of religion
- Self-incrimination
- Freedom of the press
- Eminent domain
- Right to be informed of the nature and cause of the accusation

Name: _____ Date: _____

Level Two, Lesson 4: Bill of Rights, Part II (cont.)

AMENDMENTS IN THE BILL OF RIGHTS

FIRST AMENDMENT

_____

_____

_____

_____

SECOND AMENDMENT

_____

THIRD AMENDMENT

_____

FOURTH AMENDMENT

_____

_____

_____

FIFTH AMENDMENT

_____

_____

_____

_____

SIXTH AMENDMENT

_____

_____

SEVENTH AMENDMENT

_____

EIGHTH AMENDMENT

_____

NINTH AMENDMENT

_____

TENTH AMENDMENT

_____

Name: _____ Date: _____

Level Three, Lesson 1: Baseball's Hall of Fame

Baseball's Hall of Fame

One of America's most popular tourist attractions is the National Baseball Hall of Fame in Cooperstown, New York. The Hall of Fame is an independent not-for-profit educational institution whose mission is to preserve history, honor excellence, and connect generations as they relate to baseball. Dedicated to fostering an appreciation of the historical development of baseball and to its impact on our culture, the Hall of Fame Museum collects, preserves, exhibits, and interprets artifacts from the game of baseball. The Baseball Hall of Fame also honors those who have made outstanding contributions to America's national pastime. It is one of the best-known sports shrines in the world and serves as a symbol of the most meaningful honor bestowed on an individual athlete.

Located on Main Street in a tiny, picturesque town of only 2,200 inhabitants in central New York state, the Baseball Hall of Fame attracts 400,000 visitors a year. The three-story red brick building is by far the largest repository of baseball information in the world. The museum houses more than 35,000 baseball artifacts such as bats, balls, gloves, caps, helmets, uniforms, shoes, trophies and awards, and over 130,000 baseball cards. All memorabilia in the museum's collections were donated. The Hall of Fame Library contains 2.6 million items including photographs, books, magazines, newspaper clippings, films, and video and audiotapes. The photo collection alone contains more than 500,000 historic pictures of players, teams, ballparks, and other baseball subjects. The library also maintains an extensive collection of Hollywood movies that feature baseball, such as *Field of Dreams, The Natural,* and *A League of Their Own.*

The National Baseball Hall of Fame and Museum opened its doors to the public on June 12, 1939. The first players inducted were Ty Cobb, Walter Johnson, Christy Mathewson, Babe Ruth, and Honus Wagner. Ty Cobb received the most votes. In 1962, Jackie Robinson became the first African-American elected to the Hall of Fame, and eleven years later, Roberto Clemente became the first Latin-born player to be inducted. Satchel Paige was the first Negro League player elected to the Hall of Fame in 1971. With the election of Dennis Eckersley and Paul Molitor in 2004, a total of 258 individuals have been inducted into the Hall of Fame so far, 193 of them former major league players. The plaques of the Hall of Fame members line the oak walls in the historic Hall of Fame Gallery. The Gallery serves as the centerpiece of the Baseball Hall of Fame.

The Baseball Hall of Fame stands as the definitive repository of baseball's treasures; it fuels every fan's dreams with its stories, legends, and magic passed on from generation to generation. No wonder the National Baseball Hall of Fame is such a popular tourist attraction!

Name: _____ Date: _____

Level Three, Lesson 1: Baseball's Hall of Fame (cont.)

Reading Guide for "Baseball's Hall of Fame"

BEFORE READING

Before reading "Baseball's Hall of Fame," complete the **Before Reading** section of the Reading Guide.

A. Prereading Activity: Word Search

Baseball Word Search

Directions: Find and circle the baseball words hidden in the word search below. Words may be printed forward, backward, horizontally, vertically, or diagonally.

WORD LIST
awards
Babe Ruth
ball
ballpark
baseball cards
bat
cap
Roberto Clemente
Ty Cobb
fan
first base
glove
Hall of Fame
helmet
major league
Satchel Paige
player
Jackie Robinson
spikes
sport
stadium
team
trophies
uniform

Name: _____ Date: _____

 Level Three, Lesson 1: Baseball's Hall of Fame (cont.)

B. Vocabulary: Sentences

Hall of Fame Vocabulary

Directions: Use the following words in a sentence of your own. If you are unsure about what the word means, look it up in a dictionary or online.

1. tourist: _____

_____

2. artifact: _____

_____

3. picturesque: _____

_____

4. repository: _____

_____

5. plaque: _____

_____

6. memorabilia: _____

_____

C. Prereading Questions

1. What do you think this reading is going to be about?

_____

_____

2. Read the questions in the **After Reading** section of this Reading Guide.

   a. Which question do you find the most interesting?

_____

_____

Name: _____ Date: _____

Level Three, Lesson 1: Baseball's Hall of Fame (cont.)

b.   Which answer do you think will be hardest to find?

_____

_____

3.   What is your purpose for reading this story? Finish this sentence: I am reading to find out ...

_____

_____

DURING READING

1.   Put a check mark in the margin next to the information that answers the questions in the **After Reading** section.

2.   Circle any words you don't know when you come to them in the passage.

3.   Put a question mark in the margin for anything you don't understand.

AFTER READING

1.   READING THE LINES: Answer these questions by using information in the selection.

a.   What is the official name of baseball's Hall of Fame?

_____

b.   Where is the Hall of Fame located?

_____

c.   Why is the Baseball Hall of Fame a popular tourist attraction?

_____

_____

_____

Level Three, Lesson 1: Baseball's Hall of Fame (cont.)

2. READING BETWEEN THE LINES: Answer these questions by inferring ideas in the selection.

    a.   How does the Museum preserve history?

_____

_____

Honor excellence?

_____

_____

_____

Connect generations?

_____

_____

_____

    b.   Explain this sentence in your own words: "The Baseball Hall of Fame stands as the definitive repository of baseball's treasures ..."

_____

_____

_____

    c.   Of the 258 members of the Hall of Fame, only 193 of them played in the major leagues. Who are the others?

_____

_____

_____

Level Three, Lesson 1: Baseball's Hall of Fame (cont.)

3. READING BEYOND THE LINES: Answer these questions with your own opinions.

a. Have you ever visited the Baseball Hall of Fame or another popular tourist attraction? Describe your experience.

_____

_____

_____

_____

b. For which teams did Dennis Eckersley and Paul Molitor play?

_____

_____

_____

ASSESSMENT/REINFORCEMENT

A. Go to www.baseballhalloffame.org. Click on What's New, Baseball History, or Hall of Fame Weekend. Gather the facts on a 3″ x 5″ card and report to your class.

B. Read the following paragraph about the All-American Girls Professional Baseball League. Then, using the Internet or other reference sources, answer the questions that follow for more information about the league. One useful website is: www.aagpbl.org.

The All-American Girls Professional Baseball League

By the fall of 1942, many minor league baseball teams had disbanded due to World War II. Many young men were being drafted into the armed services. In the fear that eventually the major league baseball parks would suffer severe financial losses for the same reason, Philip K. Wrigley decided to search for a solution. The All-American Girls Professional Baseball League was formed. From 1943–1954, women players from across the country entertained fans by playing baseball. The women had to follow strict rules of conduct at all times, in order to set a good example both in appearance and behavior for their fans. Each woman was expected to promote an image of "the girl next door" in spikes.

Name: _____ Date: _____

Level Three, Lesson 1: Baseball's Hall of Fame (cont.)

1. What were the names of the teams of the League that were formed during the years from 1943–1954?

2. Why were notable sports figures recruited as managers of the League teams?

3. What were some of the similarities and differences between the women's league and the men's leagues?

4. What were some of the "Rules of Conduct" the women had to follow?

5. What was the result if they broke the rules?

6. After baseball practices in the evenings during their training, why did the women have to learn how to apply makeup, how to select clothing, the proper ways of speaking and walking, and other social skills? Why was it so important that the women look and act a certain way?

7. What were some of the items in a player's "beauty kit"?

8. What does the expression, "the girl next door" mean?

9. Describe the baseball uniforms.

10. How did each team's uniforms differ?

11. At the beginning of each game during World War II, what routine was performed?

12. How did the players display their patriotism to the public outside their regular league play?

13. About how many women athletes were in the League throughout the years of 1943–1954?

14. What were the rules when the women dealt with their fans?

15. Why did the League disband?

Name: _____ Date: _____

Level Three, Lesson 2: Habitat for Humanity

Habitat for Humanity

Habitat for Humanity is a grassroots movement that seeks to eliminate poverty housing and homelessness from the world. Habitat for Humanity is trying to do something about the growing gap between the number of affordable housing units and the number of people needing them.

HFH believes that decent shelter should be a matter of conscience and action. Their goal is to build simple, decent, affordable houses for those who need them. The houses they build are simple and modestly sized; they are large enough for the family but small enough to keep construction costs down. The builders use quality materials that are locally available and that reflect the local climate and culture. All Habitat houses incorporate basic design features like wide passage doors and hallways and no-step porches that make them handicap-accessible. HFH uses future home owners and volunteers to build the houses to keep the costs down. These savings and a no-profit, no-interest loan make Habitat houses affordable for people with low incomes around the world.

The idea for Habitat resulted from a visit by Linda and Millard Fuller to a small, interracial, Christian farming community in Americus, Georgia. The founder of this community was biblical scholar and farmer, Clarence Jordan. Jordan and the Fullers developed the idea of "partnership housing"—where people in need of adequate shelter would work side by side with volunteers to build simple, decent houses. The houses would be sold at no profit and with no interest on the mortgage. Homeowners and volunteers would build the homes under the supervision of trained professionals. The funding would come from churches, corporations, individuals, and groups. Their donations, grants, and short-term loans would be put into a revolving Fund for Humanity. This Fund would provide the initial cost of building the houses. The Fund would then take in money from homeowners' house payments, donations, and no-interest loans from friends and supporters, plus money earned through fundraising activities. The money received would be used to build more houses.

"Partner families" are chosen based on their level of need, their willingness to become partners in the program, and their ability to repay the no-interest loan. HFH does not discriminate according to race, religion, gender, or ethnic group. If a family is in need of affordable housing, they contact the nearest Habitat office. Local offices then provide information on availability, size, costs, and other requirements as well as the application process.

Through the work of Habitat for Humanity, thousands of families with low incomes have found new hope in the form of affordable housing. Habitat has built and rehabilitated more than 175,000 houses for families in need. Nearly 900,000 people in 3,000 communities have been sheltered by a Habitat house. A new Habitat house is built every 26 minutes. Decent housing for all Americans should be a matter of public conscience and action. If more people of different backgrounds, races, and religions built houses together in partnership with families in need, we might eliminate homelessness in America.

Name: _____ Date: _____

Level Three, Lesson 2: Habitat for Humanity (cont.)

Reading Guide for "Habitat for Humanity"

BEFORE READING

Before reading "Habitat for Humanity," complete the **Before Reading** section of the Reading Guide.

A. Prereading Activity: What I Know About ...

Homelessness

Directions: Families with children are among the fastest-growing segments of the homeless population. What ideas do you have to eradicate homelessness in America? Write an opinion essay here about what you would do to solve the homeless situation.

_____

_____

_____

_____

_____

_____

_____

_____

_____

_____

_____

_____

Level Three, Lesson 2: Habitat for Humanity (cont.)

B. Vocabulary: Phrases

A Matter of Phrasing

Directions: Read each phrase and decide what it means. Write your response on the lines next to the phrase.

What do these mean?

1. locally available _____

_____

2. partnership housing _____

_____

3. affordable housing _____

_____

4. grass-roots movement _____

_____

5. a matter of conscience _____

_____

6. construction costs _____

_____

7. modestly sized _____

_____

8. handicap-accessible _____

_____

9. no-interest loan _____

_____

10. biblical scholar _____

_____

Name: _____ Date: _____

Level Three, Lesson 2: Habitat for Humanity (cont.)

C. Prereading Questions

1. What do you think this reading is going to be about?

   _____

   _____

2. Read the questions in the **After Reading** section of this Reading Guide.

   a.   Which question do you find the most interesting?

   _____

   _____

   b.   Which answer do you think will be hardest to find?

   _____

   _____

3. What is your purpose for reading this story? Finish this sentence: I am reading to find out ...

   _____

   _____

DURING READING

1. Put a check mark in the margin next to the information that answers the questions in the **After Reading** section.

2. Circle any words you don't know when you come to them in the passage.

3. Put a question mark in the margin for anything you don't understand.

Name: _____ Date: _____

Level Three, Lesson 2: Habitat for Humanity (cont.)

AFTER READING

1. **READING THE LINES:** Answer these questions by using information in the selection.

   a. Who were the main developers of Habitat for Humanity?

   _____

   _____

   b. What is the goal of Habitat for Humanity?

   _____

   _____

   _____

   c. What is a "partner family"?

   _____

   _____

   d. How does Habitat for Humanity keep the costs of building so low?

   _____

   _____

   _____

2. **READING BETWEEN THE LINES:** Answer these questions by inferring ideas in the selection.

   a. How would you summarize this reading?

   _____

   _____

   _____

Level Three, Lesson 2: Habitat for Humanity (cont.)

b. Do you think it is a good idea to have the future owners help out with building their homes? Why? What advantages do you see?

_____

_____

_____

_____

3. READING BEYOND THE LINES: Answer these questions with your own opinions.

a. If you and your family, or a family that you knew, was in need of low-income housing, how would you organize the application for this program? What would you say?

_____

_____

_____

_____

b. If you were on the board of directors for HFH, what would you ask each applicant?

_____

_____

_____

c. Why do you think there isn't enough housing for people with low incomes?

_____

_____

_____

_____

Level Three, Lesson 2: Habitat for Humanity (cont.)

ASSESSMENT/REINFORCEMENT

A. If you would like more information about HFH, write or phone their headquarters at:

Habitat for Humanity International
121 Habitat Street
Americus, GA 31709-3498
U.S.A.
(229) 924-6935

B. Go to www.habitat.org to find out more ways to get involved with HFH and find out how you can help eradicate homelessness.

C. Habitat for Humanity Criss-Cross Puzzle: Use a pencil for this puzzle. Using the boldface terms in the sentences below, fit them into the puzzle on the next page. Two terms may fit in the same boxes, but if you are unable to connect the next term, you know you have written in the wrong one. Erase and continue with the term that fits. The first term has been done for you. To continue, find an 18-letter term that has an "a" for the sixth letter.

6 LETTERS
Women Build's mission is to nurture, recruit, and train women to build simple, decent, healthy, and affordable **houses**.
The idea of Habitat for Humanity was developed by Linda and Millard **Fuller** and Clarence **Jordan**.

7 LETTERS
Dr. Martin Luther King, Jr.'s dream was to eliminate racism, **poverty**, and violence and is the inspiration for Habitat's Building on the Dream **program**.
One way "**partner** families" are chosen is based on their level of need.

9 LETTERS
Building on the Dream embraces and celebrates cultural diversity and religious solidarity. Dr. King referred to this as "the beloved **community**."
Habitat for Humanity greatly depends on **donations** for **materials** and labor.

10 LETTERS
A great part of Habitat for Humanity's success is its **volunteers**.
Women Build is another Habitat for Humanity program to promote the training of women in construction skills. When the women learn to build Habitat homes, it gives them **confidence** and self-esteem.

12 LETTERS
The training of women in **construction** skills empowers them to take action to move their children out of poverty.
The **headquarters** for Habitat for Humanity is in Americus, Georgia.
The funding for Habitat houses comes from churches, **corporations**, individuals, and groups.

16 LETTERS
The Building on the Dream program sponsors annual nationwide events centered around the **Martin Luther King**, Jr. holiday.

18 LETTERS
Habitat for Humanity has a program called "**Building on the Dream**."

Name: _____ Date: _____

Level Three, Lesson 2: Habitat for Humanity (cont.)

Habitat for Humanity Criss-Cross Puzzle: Use a pencil for this puzzle. Using the boldface terms in the sentences on the previous page, fit them into the puzzle below. Two terms may fit in the same boxes, but if you are unable to connect the next term, you know you have written in the wrong one. Erase and continue with the term that fits. The first term has been done for you. To continue, find an 18-letter term that has an "a" for the sixth letter.

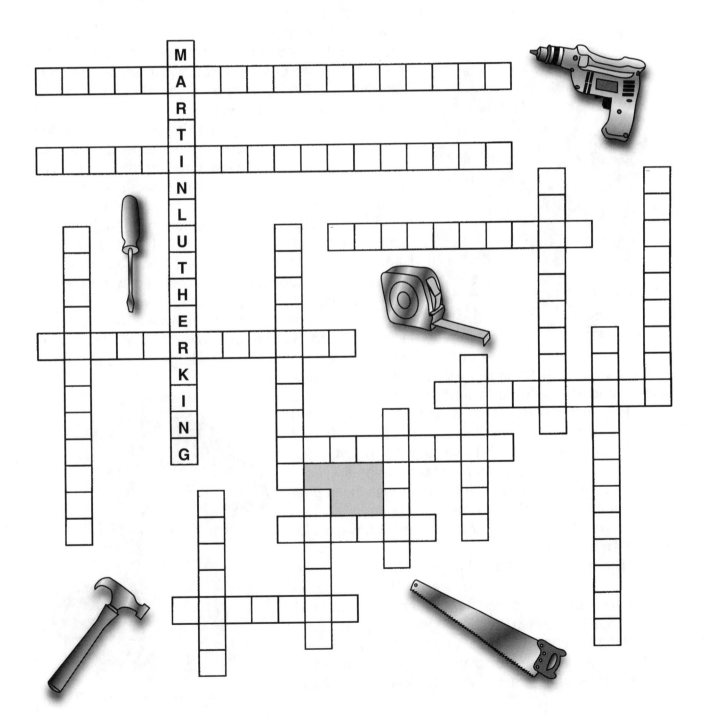

Level Three, Lesson 3: Harlem USA

Harlem USA

Harlem is a neighborhood occupying part of northern Manhattan Island in New York City. It is, perhaps, the most famous African-American community in the United States. Once a fashionable residential section of New York City, Harlem today is a depressed economic area with high rates of unemployment and substandard housing.

As a neighborhood, Harlem has no fixed boundaries. It is generally considered to lie between 155th Street on the north, the East and Harlem Rivers on the east, 96th Street, 110th Street and Cathedral Parkway on the south, and Amsterdam Avenue on the west. The chief artery of black Harlem is 125th Street, popularly called "the Main Stem" and home to the legendary Apollo Theater. Lennox Avenue was known internationally for its entertainment spots, a major Harlem tourist attraction.

Harlem was settled by the Dutch in 1658 and was named Nieuw Haarlem after Haarlem in the Netherlands. George Washington fought the British at the Battle of Harlem Heights near the spot where Columbia University now stands. Throughout the eighteenth century, Harlem was a small, rural, quiet farming community. At the turn of the century, vastly improved transportation facilities linked Harlem with lower Manhattan. It then became a residential area with large, spacious houses and many summer "cottages." Harlem attracted a large Jewish population, Italians, and Puerto Ricans and other Hispanic groups. Many apartment houses were constructed during the building boom of the 1880s but then stood vacant following the financial panic of 1893. This led property owners to rent to blacks migrating from the South. Following World War I, Harlem was the largest and most influential African-American community in the nation; it was the center of creativity and innovation for African-Americans.

There was a flowering of African-American literature, art, and music in the 1920s, mainly in Harlem. This period is called the "Harlem Renaissance." Writers like W.E.B. Du Bois, Langston Hughes, Zora Neale Hurston, and Countee Cullen flourished in the intellectual atmosphere of black Harlem. Artists such as Augusta Savage, James Van Der Zee, and William

Zora Neale Hurston

76

Name: _____ Date: _____

Level Three, Lesson 3: Harlem USA (cont.)

H. Johnson produced original works dealing with African-American life. Singer and actress Ethel Waters and comedienne Florence Mills got their start in show business on Lennox Avenue. The Apollo Theater welcomed notable performances by African-American musicians and entertainers such as Billie Holiday, Louis Armstrong, Count Basie, and Duke Ellington.

Louis Armstrong

Harlem is the site of the Abyssinian Baptist Church, the Lafayette Theatre, the Apollo Theater, and Harlem Hospital. Adam Clayton Powell, Jr., flamboyant U.S. politician, served as pastor of Abyssinian Baptist Church. Powell sponsored many pieces of legislation that improved the lives of poor blacks living in Harlem. The Lafayette Theatre, also known as "House Beautiful," was the first New York theater to desegregate. In 1912, African-American theatergoers were allowed to sit in orchestra seats and in the balcony. Harlem Hospital opened in 1887 and provided medical care for the poor. It was one of the first New York hospitals to integrate its medical staff.

Today Harlem is home to a greatly expanded black population, a large Puerto Rican community in "Spanish Harlem," and a small group of Italians in "Italian Harlem." There is considerable friction between these ethnic groups, though they share similar economic and social problems. High rates of unemployment and decrepit dwellings, as well as high rates of residential mobility, have caused severe deterioration of the neighborhood known as Harlem.

Name: _____ Date: _____

 # Level Three, Lesson 3: Harlem USA (cont.)

Reading Guide for "Harlem USA"

BEFORE READING

Before reading "Harlem USA," complete the **Before Reading** section of the Reading Guide.

A. Prereading Activity: What I Think I Know

Harlem USA

Directions: What do you know about Harlem? Put a check in front of each word or group of words that you think describes Harlem now or as it once was.

_____ 1. neighborhood   _____ 2. tourist attraction

_____ 3. fashionable   _____ 4. substandard

_____ 5. depressed   _____ 6. farming community

_____ 7. intellectuals   _____ 8. entertainers

_____ 9. artists   _____ 10. writers

_____ 11. poverty   _____ 12. unemployment

B. Vocabulary: Terms

Two-Word Phrases

Directions: Write what each of these two-word phrases means.

1. chief artery _____

_____

2. known internationally _____

_____

3. transportation facilities _____

_____

Name: _____ Date: _____

Level Three, Lesson 3: Harlem USA (cont.)

4. financial panic _____

    _____

5. intellectual atmosphere _____

    _____

6. orchestra seats _____

    _____

7. ethnic groups _____

    _____

8. decrepit dwellings _____

    _____

9. residential mobility _____

    _____

10. severe deterioration _____

    _____

C. Prereading Questions

1. What do you think this reading is going to be about?

    _____

    _____

2. Read the questions in the **After Reading** section of this Reading Guide.

    a. Which question do you find the most interesting?

        _____

        _____

Level Three, Lesson 3: Harlem USA (cont.)

b.   Which answer do you think will be hardest to find?

_____

_____

3.   What is your purpose for reading this story? Finish this sentence: I am reading to find out ...

_____

_____

DURING READING

1.   Put a check mark in the margin next to the information that answers the questions in the **After Reading** section.

2.   Circle any words you don't know when you come to them in the passage.

3.   Put a question mark in the margin for anything you don't understand.

AFTER READING

1.   READING THE LINES: Answer these questions by using information in the selection.

a.   Harlem is a
   _____ neighborhood.
   _____ island.
   _____ residence.
   _____ park.

b.   The "heart" of Harlem is
   _____ Lennox Avenue.
   _____ Cathedral Parkway.
   _____ 125th Street.
   _____ the Apollo Theater.

Level Three, Lesson 3: Harlem USA (cont.)

c.   Harlem has been home to all but which one of these ethnic groups?

_____ African-Americans

_____ Irish

_____ Italians

_____ Jewish

d.   True or False?

_____ Following World War I, Harlem was the largest and most influential African-American community in the United States.

_____ Harlem was once the center of creativity and innovation for African-Americans.

2.   READING BETWEEN THE LINES: Answer these questions by inferring ideas in the selection.

a.   What were some reasons for Harlem's decline in the twentieth century?

_____

_____

_____

_____

b.   Could this decline be reversed? How?

_____

_____

_____

_____

Level Three, Lesson 3: Harlem USA (cont.)

c. Why was the cultural boom in Harlem in the 1920s called the "Harlem Renaissance"?

_____

_____

_____

_____

3. READING BEYOND THE LINES: Answer these questions with your own opinions.

a. In your opinion, what or who contributed the most to the betterment of society during the Harlem Renaissance? Why do you think so?

_____

_____

_____

_____

_____

b. The narrative says there was considerable friction between the ethnic groups in Harlem. What reasons can you think of for why this might be true?

_____

_____

_____

_____

_____

Level Three, Lesson 3: Harlem USA (cont.)

c.   Read the poem "Harlem" by Langston Hughes, and then tell what you think the poem means.

Harlem

What happens to a dream deferred?
        Does it dry up
        like a raisin in the sun?
        Or fester like a sore—
        And then run?
        Does it stink like rotten meat?
        Or crust and sugar over—
        like a syrupy sweet?
        Maybe it just sags
        like a heavy load.
        Or does it explode?

_____

_____

_____

_____

ASSESSMENT AND REINFORCEMENT

A number of very talented African-Americans were associated with the Harlem Renaissance. Some of them are listed below. Their accomplishments were in the areas of writing, art, music, and many others. Using the Internet or other reference sources, write each name under his or her area of accomplishment on the next page. Two names will be used more than once. Then choose someone and prepare a biographical report about him or her.

W.E.B. Du Bois	Bert Williams	Zora Neale Hurston
Pops Foster	Fiorello H. LaGuardia	Langston Hughes
Aida Overton Walker	Marcus Garvey	Augusta Savage
Ralph Ellison	James Van Der Zee	Louis T. Wright
Florence Mills	Ethel Waters	Hurbert T. Delaney
Billie Holiday	Charles S. Johnson	Jessie Fauset
Count Basie	E. Franklin Frazier	Duke Ellington
Adam Clayton Powell, Jr.	Louis Armstrong	Aaron Douglas
Jacob Lawrence	Luis Russell	Claude McKay
Countee Cullen	George Walker	Fletcher Henderson

Name: _____ Date: _____

Level Three, Lesson 3: Harlem USA (cont.)

SINGERS, ACTORS, COMEDIANS

_____
_____
_____
_____
_____
_____

MUSICIANS

_____
_____
_____
_____
_____

POETS, NOVELISTS

_____
_____
_____
_____
_____
_____
_____

ARTISTS

_____
_____
_____

EDUCATORS

_____
_____
_____

POLITICIANS

_____
_____
_____

PHOTOGRAPHER

_____

LAWYER, JUDGE

_____

MEDICAL DOCTOR

_____

Name: _____   Date: _____

Level Three, Lesson 4: The Gentle Giant

The Gentle Giant: The World's Tallest Man

Who is the tallest person you've ever met? Basketball stars Shaquille O'Neal, Rebecca Lobo, and Yao Ming are all super-tall in a sport where height is an advantage. Yet, none are as tall as the World's Tallest Man, Robert Wadlow. At the time of his death, Wadlow measured 8 feet, 11 inches tall and weighed 439 pounds. For Wadlow, height was not an advantage.

Robert Pershing Wadlow was born February 22, 1918, in Alton, Illinois. He was a normal baby, weighing $8\frac{1}{2}$ pounds, and was named for General Pershing, a World War I hero. Robert was the first-born child of Addie and Harold Wadlow. He had two sisters, Helen and Betty, and two brothers, Eugene and Harold, Jr. All of Robert's siblings were of normal size; Robert, however, wasn't. His parents first suspected there might be something wrong with their son when he weighed 30 pounds at 6 months of age. At one year, he weighed 44 pounds, which is twice the normal weight of a one-year-old baby.

Doctors examined Robert and discovered he had an overactive pituitary gland; the pituitary gland is the gland that controls growth. At the time, there was no treatment or remedy to stop the growth, and Robert got bigger and bigger. At the age of nine, he was 6 feet, 2 inches tall, and at 16, he was 7 feet, 10 inches tall and weighed 400 pounds. He tried to live a normal life, but it was difficult.

As a youngster, Robert was in very good health, but his exceptionally large feet troubled him for years. At 13 he became the world's tallest Boy Scout at 7 feet, 4 inches tall. Robert collected stamps and matchbooks; he joined the YMCA, the Order of DeMolay, the Main Street Methodist Church, and the Franklin Lodge in Alton; he learned photography. He was a successful student until his college years. In 1936, at the age of 18, Robert received a scholarship from Shurtleff College in Alton. He was 8 feet, 4 inches tall at the time and weighed 390 pounds. He wanted to become an attorney. College life, however, was difficult for the Gentle Giant. The pens and pencils were difficult to hold, and the lab instruments were a nightmare to use. Robert had difficulty walking in icy conditions and had trouble moving from building to building between classes. His medical condition also made his bones brittle and easily broken. Robert gave up his dream of becoming an attorney and dropped out of college.

Name: _____ Date: _____

Level Three, Lesson 4: The Gentle Giant (cont.)

At the age of 20, Robert Wadlow became a goodwill ambassador for the International Shoe Company who made his size 37 shoes. With his father, Robert toured the country promoting the Company. His father modified the family car by removing the front passenger seat so Robert could sit in the back seat and stretch out his long legs. Together they visited over 800 towns and 41 states and traveled over 300,000 miles. As part of the promotion, Wadlow would leave behind his own shoes for store owners to display. He then received his new shoes, free of charge, from the company.

Robert Wadlow had trouble with his big feet. He had little sensation or feeling in his feet and toes. He couldn't feel his shoes rub against his feet until blisters formed. While on tour in Michigan, he developed blisters on his feet, which then became infected. Doctors performed surgery and administered blood transfusions, but the infection lingered. He passed away on July 15, 1940.

The Gentle Giant was returned to Alton for burial. His parents buried their son under a vault of concrete in the fear that his body would be unearthed and examined for medical research. It took 12 pallbearers plus an additional eight men to carry the 1,000-pound casket. His father and mother had most of Robert's belongings destroyed; they did not want collectors to obtain his clothes and other personal items and display them in "freak" shows. On the day of his burial, businesses in Alton closed as a sign of respect for the World's Tallest Man. Forty thousand people attended Robert's funeral.

In 1985, a life-sized bronze statue was erected in Alton as a tribute to Robert P. Wadlow. The tallest man in history was a kind, thoughtful, gentle person who loved his mother deeply. He is remembered as a quiet young man who overcame a unique handicap and was an inspiration to all who knew him.

Name: _____ Date: _____

Level Three, Lesson 4: The Gentle Giant (cont.)

Reading Guide for "The Gentle Giant"

BEFORE READING

Before reading "The Gentle Giant," complete the **Before Reading** section of the Reading Guide.

A. Prereading Activity: Building Bridges

Giant

Directions: Examine the drawing carefully. Who is the statue of? What do you know about this person?

ROBERT PERSHING WADLOW

_____

_____

_____

Name: _____ Date: _____

Level Three, Lesson 4: The Gentle Giant (cont.)

B. Vocabulary: Antonyms

Giant Vocabulary

Directions: Write an antonym in the box next to the vocabulary words.

a. tall		b. difficult	
c. advantage		d. bigger	
e. hero		f. overactive	
g. wrong		h. son	
i. nightmare		j. walking	
k. goodwill		l. father	
m. sit		n. destroy	
o. kind		p. thoughtful	
q. gentle		r. quiet	
s. young		t. tribute	

C. Prereading Questions

1. What do you think this reading is going to be about?

    _____

    _____

2. Read the questions in the **After Reading** section of this Reading Guide.

    a.   Which question do you find the most interesting?

        _____

        _____

    b.   Which answer do you think will be hardest to find?

        _____

        _____

Name: _____ Date: _____

Level Three, Lesson 4: The Gentle Giant (cont.)

3. What is your purpose for reading this story? Finish this sentence: I am reading to find out ...

_____

_____

DURING READING

1. Put a check mark in the margin next to the information that answers the questions in the **After Reading** section.

2. Circle any words you don't know when you come to them in the passage.

3. Put a question mark in the margin for anything you don't understand.

AFTER READING

1. READING THE LINES: Answer these questions by using information in the selection.

   a. Who is the tallest person you have ever met?

   _____

   b. Why was being tall a disadvantage for Robert?

   _____

   _____

   c. What kind of problems did Robert have with his feet?

   _____

   _____

   _____

   d. Where did Robert get his shoes made?

   _____

Name: _____ Date: _____

Level Three, Lesson 4: The Gentle Giant (cont.)

2. READING BETWEEN THE LINES: Answer these questions by inferring ideas in the selection.

   a. Why was life so difficult for Robert Wadlow?

   _____

   _____

   _____

   b. How would Robert Wadlow's life be different if he was born today?

   _____

   _____

   _____

   c. What is a goodwill ambassador?

   _____

   _____

   d. Do you think Wadlow's parents were justified in their fears? Why?

   _____

   _____

   _____

3. READING BEYOND THE LINES: Answer these questions with your own opinions.

   a. How many of your feet would fit a size 37 shoe?

   _____

   b. Who are some tall people of the modern era?

   _____

   _____

Level Three, Lesson 4: The Gentle Giant (cont.)

c. How old was Robert Wadlow when he died?

_____

d. Compare your height and weight at age 12 with Robert's: height 6´11˝, weight 241 pounds.

_____

_____

ASSESSMENT/REINFORCEMENT

A. To learn more about the Gentle Giant, read *Boy Giant* by Dan Brannan or visit the Alton Museum of History and Art.

B. Robert Wadlow's Life: Look up Robert Pershing Wadlow on the Internet, and then put the facts below in chronological order.

_____ 1. Robert took his first airplane ride; he had his first checkup at Barnes Hospital in St. Louis, where his family learned of his overactive pituitary gland.

_____ 2. Robert dies as a result of an infection from blisters on his feet, caused by the lack of sensation in his feet.

_____ 3. In kindergarten, Robert was 5 feet, $6\frac{1}{2}$ inches tall. He wore clothes that would have fit a 17-year-old boy.

_____ 4. Robert graduated from Alton High School.

_____ 5. Robert was born on February 22, 1918, to Harold and Addie Wadlow in Alton, Illinois.

_____ 6. When Robert began to walk, he weighed 40 pounds.

_____ 7. Robert traveled with his father as a goodwill ambassador for International Shoe Company.

_____ 8. Robert enrolled in Shurtleff College.

Level Three, Lesson 4: The Gentle Giant (cont.)

_____ 9. At the age of 13, Robert was the largest Boy Scout in the world. It took 14 yards of 36-inch-wide material to make his uniform.

_____ 10. Robert attended the World's Fair in Chicago. It took two turns and 20¢ to get him through the turnstile.

_____ 11. Robert sold magazines to earn money for a savings account. When the banks failed, he lost his savings.

_____ 12. At 10 years old, Robert weighed 210 pounds and was 6 feet, 5 inches tall. His shoes were size $17\frac{1}{2}$.

C. If Robert were alive today and you were assigned to interview him, what questions would you ask him?

1. _____

   _____

2. _____

   _____

3. _____

   _____

4. _____

   _____

5. _____

   _____

Level Four, Lesson 1: Life in the Desert

Life in the Desert

Deserts are barren regions that support very little plant and animal life; what life there is has adapted to the conditions of the desert. Second only to tropical rain forests, deserts support a wide variety of plant and animal life. Desert animals have adapted to the lack of water, the extreme temperatures, and the shortage of food. Many desert animals are nocturnal—they burrow during the day and are active at night when the temperatures are cooler. Desert plants have adapted to the heat, cold, and lack of precipitation in the desert.

Animals of the Desert

Some animals can live in the extreme conditions of the desert, like the kangaroo, the camel, and the gazelle. They are big animals that can travel long distances for water. Camels store water and food in their humps, which is why they can travel such long distances. Another fairly large desert animal is the addax, often called a desert antelope. The addax lives in the Sahara. Other large animals include bighorn sheep, bobcats, coyotes, and dingoes. Bighorn sheep are wild, brown sheep found in the mountains and deserts of North America along with bobcats, short-tailed wildcats. Coyotes are found in American deserts. Dingoes are wild dogs found in the deserts of Australia.

Addax

Certain reptiles, mammals, birds, fish, and amphibians thrive in the harsh conditions of the desert. Boa constrictors, rattlesnakes, geckos, Gila monsters, and the blue-tongued skink are some of the snakes and lizards living in deserts. A boa constrictor is a large snake found in South American deserts. Rattlesnakes are venomous snakes that have a rattle at the end of their tails. Snakes rarely drink water; instead, they get their moisture from the food they eat.

Fennec Fox

Lizards stay out of the sun and move as little as possible. A Gila monster is a large, slow-moving, venomous lizard that can live months without food; it lives off the fat stored in its tail. Gila monsters are found in the Mohave, Sonoran, and Chihuahuan deserts. Geckos are nocturnal animals that have large eyes and excellent vision. These lizards make a squeaky or clicking noise that sounds like "gecko." A blue-tongued skink is an Australian lizard with a long, blue tongue.

Other interesting animals of the desert are the fennec fox, the jerboa, the Mongolian gerbil, and the mongoose. The fennec fox lives in the Sahara and is a small, desert fox

Level Four, Lesson 1: Life in the Desert (cont.)

with very large ears. It eats mice, small birds, lizards, and insects. A jerboa is a small, long-tailed rodent that lives in the desert. Jerboas are about the size of a mouse but can jump very long distances. They eat plants, seeds, and bugs. The Mongolian gerbil is a small, burrowing rodent, native to the dry, sandy deserts of Africa, the Middle East, and Asia. These mammals live together in large colonies; they are the same type of gerbils people often keep for pets. Mongooses are small, meat-eating mammals with sleek bodies, tapered snouts, sharp teeth, short feet, and long tails. They have sharp claws for digging burrows and scratching the ground for insects to eat. Mongooses are found in the scrublands of Africa and Asia.

Plants of the Desert

A variety of plants grow in the desert, though they are usually widely scattered due to the lack of water. Plants that do survive compete for the small amount of water that is available. During the day, the plant's stomata, or pores, close to prevent evaporation. Some plants store water in their leaves, roots, and stems. Woody desert plants have long root systems that reach deep water sources, while others have spreading shallow roots that are able to take in surface moisture quickly from heavy dews and occasional rains. Desert plants also tend to have small leaves. During dry periods, many plants drop their leaves on the ground.

The deserts are rich in wildflowers like the Apache plume, the Arizona poppy, the desert paintbrush, the desert lily, and the devil's claw. The wildflower datura is a sprawling poisonous perennial with long, gray-green leaves. All parts of this poisonous plant can be fatal if ingested.

The desert is home to a wide variety of cacti. The saguaro cactus, native to the Sonoran Desert, stores all of its water in its stem. Fruit from the saguaro is used to make jam, and the woody inside of the cactus is used in building materials. The barrel cactus swells with water after rainfall and shrinks as it uses its water. The old man cactus has a white hairy "head" that helps the plant reflect the hot sun. Prickly pear cacti, abundant in the Chihuahuan Desert, uses its thorns to keep animals away. Animals want to eat the cactus for the water stored in its leaves. The fishhook cactus has fishhook-shaped spines, which help divert the heat and shade the growing tip of the plant. Other hot desert plants are yuccas, ocotillo, turpentine bushes, false mesquite, sotol, ephedras, agaves, and brittle bushes.

Cold deserts support almost no vegetation because of freezing temperatures and ice. Since there is no soil, only plants that can live on rocks live in these frigid deserts. Semiarid deserts support various grasses, sagebrush, shad scale, pistachio trees, and shrubs.

Name: _____ Date: _____

Level Four, Lesson 1: Life in the Desert (cont.)

Reading Guide for "Life In the Desert"

BEFORE READING

Before reading "Life in the Desert," complete the **Before Reading** section of the Reading Guide.

A. Prereading Activity: Exploring What Is Known

Life in the Desert

Directions: Draw a picture of a desert including any plant, animal, or human life that might be found there.

Compare your drawing to the drawings of your classmates. Make a composite list of plants, animals, and humans that you think live in the desert. Then, all together, compose a three-sentence paragraph that describes a desert.

Name: _____ Date: _____

Level Four, Lesson 1: Life in the Desert (cont.)

B. Vocabulary: Exploring Meanings

Which Word Fits?

> **WORD BANK**
>
> | | | | |
> |---|---|---|---|
> | barren | frigid | rodent | tropical |
> | nocturnal | ingested | pistachio | addax |

Directions: Choose a word from the Word Bank that is in some way related to the numbered words.

1. rat   _____

2. Hawaii   _____

3. night   _____

4. eaten   _____

5. freezing   _____

6. desolate   _____

7. nut   _____

8. desert antelope   _____

C. Prereading Questions

1. What do you think this reading is going to be about?

   _____

   _____

2. Read the questions in the **After Reading** section of this Reading Guide.

   a. Which question do you find the most interesting?

   _____

   _____

Level Four, Lesson 1: Life in the Desert (cont.)

b.   Which answer do you think will be hardest to find?

_____

_____

3.   What is your purpose for reading this story? Finish this sentence: I am reading to find out ...

_____

_____

DURING READING

1.   Put a check mark in the margin next to the information that answers the questions in the **After Reading** section.

2.   Circle any words you don't know when you come to them in the passage.

3.   Put a question mark in the margin for anything you don't understand.

AFTER READING

1.   READING THE LINES: Answer these questions by using information in the selection.

a.   How many prepositions are in the first paragraph of this reading? Which one is most frequently used?

_____

_____

b.   What does the word *venomous* mean?

_____

_____

Level Four, Lesson 1: Life in the Desert (cont.)

c.   What wildflowers grow in the desert?

_____

_____

_____

d.   What is another word for *stomata*?

_____

2.   READING BETWEEN THE LINES: Answer these questions by inferring ideas in the selection.

a.   What is the main idea of this reading?

_____

_____

_____

_____

b.   What is a Gila monster, and how do you think it got its name?

_____

_____

_____

c.   What does *sprawling* mean? What are some other things that could be sprawling?

_____

_____

_____

Level Four, Lesson 1: Life in the Desert (cont.)

d.   Use the word *perennial* in a sentence of your own.

_____

_____

_____

3.   READING BEYOND THE LINES: Answer these questions with your own opinions.

a.   Have you ever been to a desert? Which one(s)? What did you see?

_____

_____

_____

b.   Cacti of the desert often have very colorful names. Draw a picture in each box of what you think each of these cacti look like.

Barrel Cactus	Old Man Cactus

Name: _____ Date: _____

Level Four, Lesson 1: Life in the Desert (cont.)

Prickly Pear Cactus	Fishhook Cactus

ASSESSMENT/REINFORCEMENT

A. People of the desert are similar to plants and animals of the desert in that they have adapted their way of life to the harsh conditions. People live in almost every desert of the world. Do some research and write an interesting narrative on the lives of one of these groups.

B. Fill in the Blanks: For the paragraph about living in the desert on the next page, fill in the words from the Word Bank below. One word will be used twice. Use the Internet or other reference sources if you need help.

WORD BANK

adapted	Apache	Bedouins	Bushmen	cacti
copper	endangered	environment	grazing	Indian
inhabited	irrigation	minerals	mining	Mongols
nomadic	people	resources	southwestern	support
survival	survive	tribes	water	

Level Four, Lesson 1: Life in the Desert (cont.)

FILL IN THE BLANKS: LIFE IN THE DESERT

Wild animals and plants have _____ for _____ in the deserts of the world. _____ have also learned how to live in the deserts. People of the desert usually live in small family groups, or _____. They are often _____—that is, they travel in search of _____, game, and forage for their animals. They camp in one particular spot for only as long as the area's limited _____ will _____ them. These wanderers are called _____ in North Africa and _____ in Australia. Some of the _____ of Central Asia are also nomadic. In the Americas, various _____ tribes chose the desert as a place to live. This may have been as a defense against other tribes who _____ the lusher biomes of the area. In the deserts of the _____ United States, we find the Pueblo, Navajo, _____, and Papago Indians.

Modern people are moving into the desert biomes. Desert sands can grow good crops if _____ can be made available. This is done through _____ canals and deeply drilled wells. Some desert regions are also rich in _____ such as gold, silver, and _____. _____ activities utilize large tracts of desert lands, as does the _____ of domestic livestock. Some _____ have become collectors' items and are disappearing from their natural _____.

Some desert land should be set aside for the future, so endangered desert species will be able to _____. Some of these _____ species are the desert bighorn ram, the kit fox, and the Gila monster.

Name: _____ Date: _____

Level Four, Lesson 2: Tuskegee Airmen

Tuskegee Airmen

The Tuskegee Airmen were African-American fighter pilots, trained at the Tuskegee Institute, who made important contributions toward winning World War II. They were the first black pilots to qualify as military pilots in any branch of the United States Armed Forces and opened the doors of opportunity for other African-Americans.

Prior to World War II, African-Americans were barred from flying for the U.S. military. The black press, the NAACP, and other black organizations put pressure on the U.S. government to train black pilots for service in World War II. In 1940, the military began making plans for a segregated air unit.

Tuskegee Institute in Alabama had a well-respected aeronautical engineering program. Because of this flight program, the United States military selected Tuskegee as a place to train African-American pilots for the war. The Tuskegee Institute was a vocational school for African-Americans founded in 1881 by Booker T. Washington. The school had technical courses such as carpentry, masonry, blacksmithing, and housekeeping. Tuskegee also trained teachers, tradesmen, and farmers. Tuskegee University today is a nationally renowned center of learning and a major political force in America.

Tuskegee was a good place for aviation training. First, it was located in the deep South, so it had excellent weather for year-round flying. Second, there was a lot of underdeveloped land for use as airfields. Third, aviation fit with the school's strong focus on vocational education, and finally, the school had a credible reputation. Booker T. Washington described Tuskegee as "a veritable cathedral of practical learning and black self-help."

By March 1942, the first African-Americans had earned their wings, and by June 9, 1943, black fighter pilots were engaging in aerial combat. Of the 1,000 African-Americans who completed the training and earned their pilot's wings, 445 went overseas as combat pilots in Europe, North Africa, and the Mediterranean. These pilots became the 99th Fighter Squadron. It was the job of the 99th to fly "bombing escort" for the heavy bomber planes and to provide a ground attack. They flew more than 15,000 missions, destroyed over 111 German planes in the air, another 150 on the ground, and destroyed 950 railcars, trucks, and other motor vehicles. None of the bombers they escorted were lost to enemy fighters. The 99th Fighter Squadron performed remarkable feats of patriotism and bravery. Of the 445 men, 66 were killed in action, and 32 pilots were shot down and captured as prisoners of war (POWs).

The Tuskegee Airmen, a collective term for the military pilots, flight engineers, gunners, mechanics, armorers, navigators, and bombardiers, continued to fight and fly until the war was won. These remarkable men earned 744 air medals, 8 Purple Hearts, and 15 Bronze Stars. They received more than 150 Distinguished Flying Crosses as a group. More importantly, the Tuskegee Airmen earned the respect of the Armed Forces and opened the door of opportunity for other African-Americans.

Tuskegee Airman being given awards

Level Four, Lesson 2: Tuskegee Airmen (cont.)

Reading Guide for "Tuskegee Airmen"

BEFORE READING

Before reading "Tuskegee Airmen," complete the **Before Reading** section of the Reading Guide.

A. Prereading Activity: Background Knowledge

Tuskegee University

Directions: Go to the website for Tuskegee University and search for answers to the questions.

www.tuskegee.edu

1. What is the "official" name of the College? _____

2. When was the University founded? _____

3. Who was the first president of the University? _____

4. Where is Tuskegee University located? _____

5. Who were the Tuskegee Airmen? _____

   _____

   _____

6. What does the inscription at the base of the Booker T. Washington Monument say?

   _____

   _____

   _____

7. Who is the current president of Tuskegee? _____

8. How many students go to Tuskegee? _____

9. How big is the campus? _____

10. What role did George Campbell and Lewis Adams play in the establishment of Tuskegee?

    _____

    _____

    _____

    _____

Name: _____ Date: _____

Level Four, Lesson 2: Tuskegee Airmen (cont.)

B. Vocabulary: Adjectives

What Is ...?

Directions: Most of the vocabulary words below should be familiar to you. However, with the addition of the adjective, the meaning shifts. Give the definition for each term.

What is ...

1. a fighter pilot? _____

_____

2. a black pilot? _____

_____

3. a combat pilot? _____

_____

4. a military pilot? _____

_____

5. a segregated air unit? _____

_____

6. an aeronautical engineering program? _____

_____

7. a technical course? _____

_____

8. aviation training? _____

_____

9. a major political force? _____

_____

10. a credible reputation? _____

_____

Name: _____ Date: _____

Level Four, Lesson 2: Tuskegee Airmen (cont.)

C. Prereading Questions

1. What do you think this reading is going to be about?

   _____

   _____

2. Read the questions in the **After Reading** section of this Reading Guide.

   a. Which question do you find the most interesting?

   _____

   _____

   b. Which answer do you think will be hardest to find?

   _____

   _____

3. What is your purpose for reading this story? Finish this sentence: I am reading to find out ...

   _____

   _____

DURING READING

1. Put a check mark in the margin next to the information that answers the questions in the **After Reading** section.

2. Circle any words you don't know when you come to them in the passage.

3. Put a question mark in the margin for anything you don't understand.

Name: _____ Date: _____

Level Four, Lesson 2: Tuskegee Airmen (cont.)

AFTER READING

1. READING THE LINES: Answer these questions by using information in the selection.

   a. Who were the Tuskegee Airmen?

   _____

   _____

   _____

   b. Why did the government choose Tuskegee?

   _____

   _____

   _____

   c. How did Booker T. Washington describe Tuskegee?

   _____

   _____

   _____

   d. What is aerial combat?

   _____

   _____

   _____

2. READING BETWEEN THE LINES: Answer these questions by inferring ideas in the selection.

   a. What is the main idea of this reading?

   _____

   _____

   _____

Level Four, Lesson 2: Tuskegee Airmen (cont.)

b. Why weren't African-Americans allowed to fly for the military prior to World War II?

_____

_____

c. What were some of the aircrew and groundcrew duties of the Tuskegee Airmen?

_____

_____

_____

d. How did the Tuskegee Airmen distinguish themselves in the war?

_____

_____

_____

3. READING BEYOND THE LINES: Answer these questions with your own opinions.

a. What were the results of the "Tuskegee Experiment"?

_____

_____

_____

b. After their training as pilots, did the Tuskegee Airmen continue to experience discrimination? If so, how?

_____

_____

_____

Level Four, Lesson 2: Tuskegee Airmen (cont.)

c. In your opinion, did the first black military aviators have it better or worse than their white counterparts? Why or why not?

_____

_____

_____

ASSESSMENT/REINFORCEMENT

A. There are a number of websites dedicated to the Tuskegee Airmen. Research some additional facts (and photographs) of the Tuskegee Airmen. Create a display for your classroom.

B. Tuskegee Airmen Criss-Cross Puzzle: Use a pencil for this puzzle. Using the boldface terms in the paragraphs below, fit them into the puzzle on the next page. Count the letters in each term and fit it into its own place in the puzzle. Two terms may fit in the same boxes, but if you are unable to connect the next term, you know you have written in the wrong one. Erase and continue with another term that fits. The first term has been done for you. To continue, find a seven-letter term that ends in "r."

During **World War II**, the **Tuskegee** Airmen gained a **champion** for their cause—President Roosevelt's wife, **Eleanor**. She opposed **racial** discrimination and supported African-Americans' rights. She went to a meeting being held by the Julius Rosenwald Fund of Chicago's board of **directors** to learn more about African-American **pilots**. The Tuskegee **Institute** had appealed to the Fund for additional **financing** of an **airfield** that was under construction.

Arriving at Tuskegee Institute on April 19, 1941, Mrs. Roosevelt **surprised** everyone by asking Chief Anderson of the Tuskegee Airmen to take her for an airplane ride. People were **amazed** that the **First Lady** would take such a risk. Some of the board members and the **Secret Service** agents who were assigned to **protect** her wanted to call the president to stop her. Ignoring their protests, she climbed into the airplane and went for a thirty-minute **flight**. When they landed, Mrs. **Roosevelt** proudly proclaimed to the press, "Well, he can fly all right!"

The First Lady set an example with her **courage** and **support** and the fact that she trusted her life to the **flying** skills of an **African-American** pilot. The **Rosenwald Fund** donated $175,000 of the $200,000 needed to **complete** the airfield.

Name: _____   Date: _____

Level Four, Lesson 2: Tuskegee Airmen (cont.)

Tuskegee Airmen Criss-Cross Puzzle: Use a pencil for this puzzle. Using the boldface terms in the paragraphs on the previous page, fit them into the puzzle below. Count the letters in each term and fit it into its own place in the puzzle. Two terms may fit in the same boxes, but if you are unable to connect the next term, you know you have written in the wrong one. Erase and continue with another term that fits. The first term has been done for you. To continue, find a seven-letter term that ends in "r."

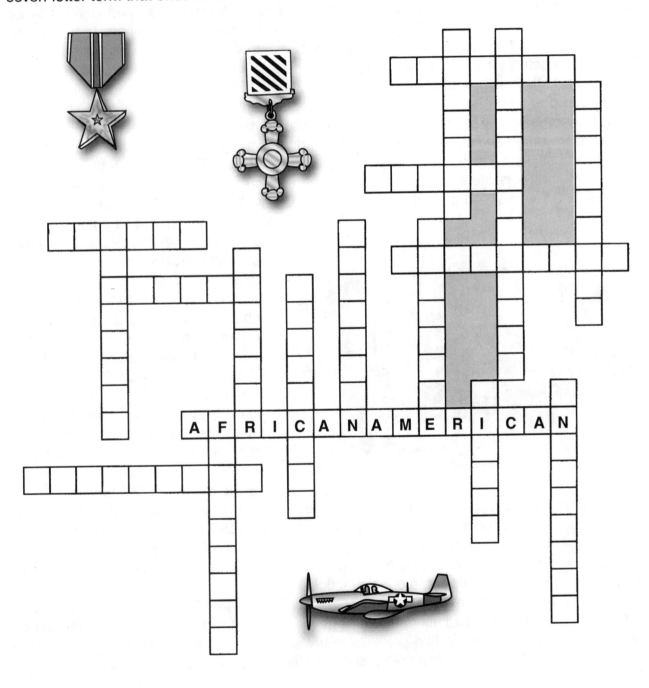

Name: _____ Date: _____

Level Four, Lesson 3: The Choctaw

The Choctaw

The tribe had been traveling through rough and dense forest for months, carrying the heavy bones of their ancestors. This task was taking its toll on the living who grew more fatigued with each passing day. The journey seems endless when you are tired and hungry. One day the People came upon a favorable creek, and the Chief decided to use the area for their winter encampment. When warmer weather came, the tribe was healthy from rest and an abundance of food in the area. The People decided to stay beside the creek permanently. So begins the story of the origin of a proud and noble people, the Choctaw.

The Choctaw Indians originated in the Mississippi Valley area in what is today southern Alabama and Mississippi and parts of Louisiana. Originally, they were part of the Muskogean tribe, and at one time were connected to the Chickasaw tribe. The Choctaw were among the first Native Americans to assimilate European-style customs, including the wearing of gowns by the Choctaw women and suits by the men. The Choctaw were known for their beautiful pottery and artistic basketry. They built roads, schools, and churches. They had a representational government, were farmers, and owned plantations. Some of the Choctaw were doctors, teachers, and lawyers, and a number of them attended "white" universities to earn degrees.

The history of a People is told by those who survive. In 1540, the giant Chief of the Choctaw, Toscalusa, also called the "Black Warrior," opposed de Soto's march into their territory in what was, perhaps, the most terrible Indian battle ever fought in the eastern United States. In 1786, the Choctaw made their first treaty with the government, and by 1820, had sold off all of "their" land. Ten years later, they were forcibly relocated from their homeland to the Oklahoma territory. 20,000 Choctaws began the forced march to Oklahoma, but only 7,000 survived it. Many Choctaw died from disease, famine, and attacks from unscrupulous white men and hostile Indians, particularly the Comanche. In Oklahoma, the Choctaw adapted to the white culture with the help of missionaries. They learned a new religion and a new value system. They adopted a new educational system, a new constitution, and a legal system. They modified their agriculture and commercial practices.

Today there are approximately 85,000 Choctaw Indians living in southeastern Oklahoma under their own written constitutional form of government ratified by the Choctaw People on July 9, 1983. The Choctaw Nation provides many services for the People including housing programs, medical services, job training, and educational programs. The Nation has become

Name: _____ Date: _____

Level Four, Lesson 3: The Choctaw (cont.)

deeply involved in economic developmental enterprises such as bingo palaces, smoke shops, and shopping centers; these economic endeavors provide numerous jobs for the Choctaw People.

The Choctaw Nation hosts the Annual Choctaw Labor Day Celebration, one of the largest and most well-known events in Oklahoma. This celebration has become a continuing tradition among the Choctaw People who host thousands of visitors on the grounds of the Historic Council House. Traditional cultural activities, arts and crafts and food, as well as sporting games, camping, fishing, and musical entertainment are just a few of the events featured at the celebration. Some of the highlights are the numerous family reunions, the Annual Choctaw Princess Pageant, the "State of the Nation Address" by Chief Gregory E. Pyle to the Choctaw People, and the introduction of the many celebrities, entertainers, and tribal leaders who attend and/or contribute to the activities.

The Choctaw Nation of Oklahoma believes that responsibility for the well-being of its members rests with the members and is governed by the Tribe. By planning and implementing its own programs and by building a strong economic base, the Choctaw Nation applies its own fiscal, natural, and human resources to develop a strong and self-sufficient community.

Name: _____   Date: _____

Level Four, Lesson 3: The Choctaw (cont.)

Reading Guide for "The Choctaw"

BEFORE READING

Before reading "The Choctaw," complete the **Before Reading** section of the Reading Guide.

A. Prereading Activity: Connecting Knowledge

Directions: Read this preamble to the Native American Commandments. Decide how a person who follows these precepts would act. On your own paper, write a list of "rules" in your own words for the behaviors contained in this statement.

- Treat the Earth and all that dwell thereon with respect.

- Remain close to the Great Spirit.

- Show great respect for your fellow beings.

- Work together for the benefit of all Mankind.

- Give assistance and kindness wherever needed.

- Do what you know to be right.

- Look after the well-being of mind and body.

- Dedicate a share of your efforts to the greater good.

- Be truthful and honest at all times.

- Take full responsibility for your actions.

For more information, check this website: www.indigenouspeople.net/tencomm.htm

Level Four, Lesson 3: The Choctaw (cont.)

B.   Vocabulary: Word Meaning

The Choctaw

Directions: Write the pronunciation and definition for each of these words.

1. fatigued   _____

    _____

2. encampment   _____

    _____

3. assimilate   _____

    _____

4. unscrupulous   _____

    _____

5. enterprise   _____

    _____

6. endeavor   _____

    _____

C.   Prereading Questions

1. What do you think this reading is going to be about?

    _____

    _____

2. Read the questions in the **After Reading** section of this Reading Guide.

    a.   Which question do you find the most interesting?

         _____

         _____

Name: _____   Date: _____

Level Four, Lesson 3: The Choctaw (cont.)

b. Which answer do you think will be hardest to find?

_____

_____

3. What is your purpose for reading this story? Finish this sentence: I am reading to find out ...

_____

_____

DURING READING

1. Put a check mark in the margin next to the information that answers the questions in the **After Reading** section.

2. Circle any words you don't know when you come to them in the passage.

3. Put a question mark in the margin for anything you don't understand.

AFTER READING

1. READING THE LINES: Answer these questions by using information in the selection.

   a. Why did the People decide to live permanently beside the "favorable creek"?

   _____

   _____

   b. Who was the "Black Warrior"?

   _____

   c. How many Choctaw survived the forced march to Oklahoma?

   _____

   _____

Name: _____ Date: _____

Level Four, Lesson 3: The Choctaw (cont.)

    d.   Who is the current Chief of the Choctaw Nation?

_____

2.   READING BETWEEN THE LINES: Answer these questions by inferring ideas in the selection.

    a.   Why do you think the government wanted the Choctaw to move off their land?

_____

_____

_____

    b.   Why were the Choctaw so successful in adapting to another culture?

_____

_____

_____

    c.   What do you think the objectives are for the Annual Choctaw Labor Day Celebration?

_____

_____

_____

3.   READING BEYOND THE LINES: Answer these questions with your own opinions.

    a.   Would you like to attend the Annual Choctaw Labor Day Celebration? Why or why not?

_____

_____

_____

Name: _____ Date: _____

Level Four, Lesson 3: The Choctaw (cont.)

b.   Has the "white man" been successful in assimilating the Choctaw into the main-stream culture? Explain.

_____

_____

_____

_____

c.   Name three famous Native Americans of the modern era.

_____

_____

ASSESSMENT/REINFORCEMENT

A. Read the entire text of the Native American Commandments at www.indigenouspeople.net/tencomm.htm. Discuss with others what they mean, and then translate them into your own words. Compare them to the Ten Commandments in the Bible. How are they the same; how are they different?

B. **Native Americans: Living Off the Land:** Using the words in each of the Word Banks below, fill in the words under the various headings on the next pages, showing how Native Americans used all available resources to live off the land.

FOREST/PLAINS WORD BANK (for page 117)

Bear	Bear Claw	Blankets	Bones	Clothing
Deer	Farming Tools	Feathers	Firewood	Furniture
Heat	Ornamentation	Raccoon	Shelter	Skins
Squirrel	To Groom Skin & Hair	Weapons		

IN OR ALONG RIVERS AND STREAMS WORD BANK (for page 118)

Axes	Baskets	Beans	Blowguns	Building
Crops	Fish	Food	Grasses	Hoes
Hunting	Pumpkins	Skins	Sweet Potatoes	Tomahawks
Tools	Trading/Bartering	Weapons		

Name: _____   Date: _____

Level Four, Lesson 3: The Choctaw (cont.)

Directions: Native Americans lived off the land, not wasting any part of it. Fill in the flow chart that illustrates this, using the words in the Word Bank on the previous page.

FORESTS/PLAINS

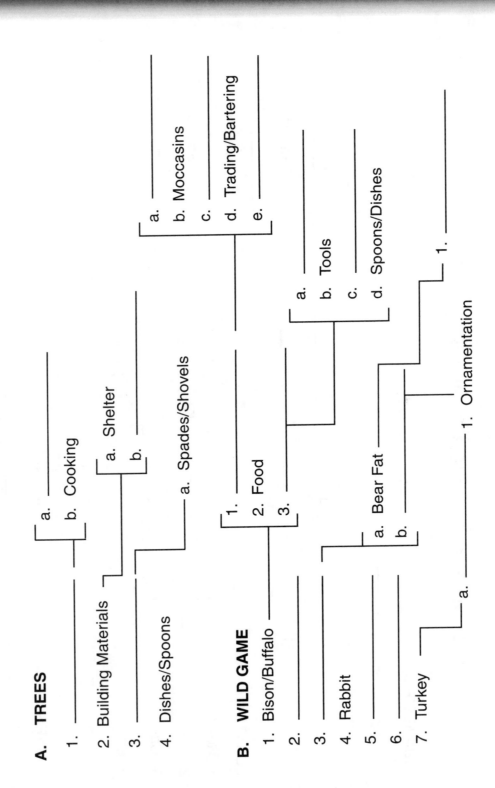

A. TREES

1. _____
   - a. _____
   - b. Cooking

2. Building Materials
   - a. Shelter
   - b. _____

3. _____

4. Dishes/Spoons
   - a. Spades/Shovels

B. WILD GAME

1. Bison/Buffalo
2. _____
   - a. _____
   - b. Moccasins
   - c. _____
   - d. Trading/Bartering
   - e. _____
3. _____
4. Rabbit
5. Bear Fat
   - a. _____
   - b. Tools
   - c. _____
   - d. Spoons/Dishes
6. _____
   - a. _____
7. Turkey
   - 1. _____
   - 1. Ornamentation

Name: _____ Date: _____

Level Four, Lesson 3: The Choctaw (cont.)

Directions: Indians lived off the land, not wasting any part of it. Fill in the flow chart that illustrates this, using the words in the Word Bank on page 116.

IN OR ALONG RIVERS AND STREAMS

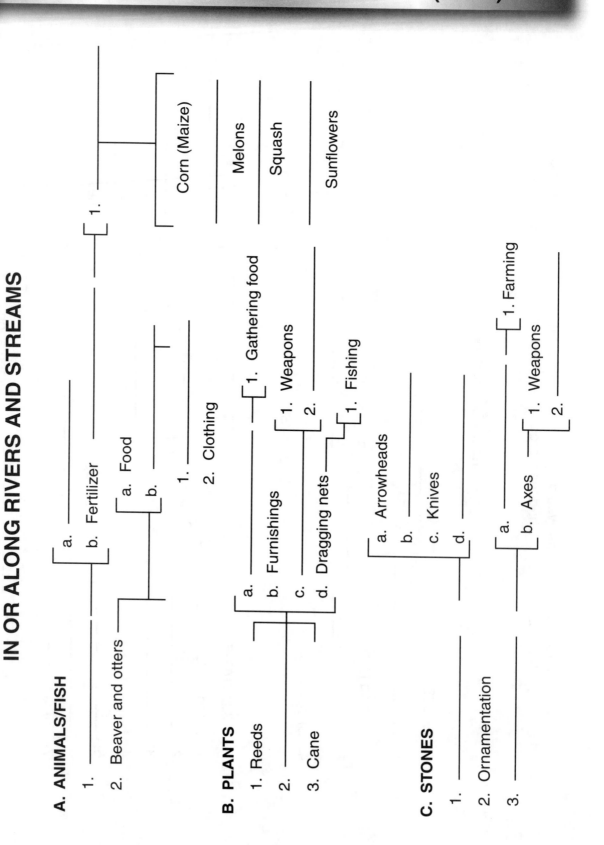

A. ANIMALS/FISH

1. _____
   - a. _____
   - b. Fertilizer
     - 1. _____
       - Corn (Maize)
       - Melons
       - Squash
       - Sunflowers
2. Beaver and otters
   - a. Food
   - b. _____
     - 1. _____
   - 2. Clothing

B. PLANTS

1. Reeds
   - a. _____
     - 1. Gathering food
   - b. Furnishings
   - c. _____
     - 1. Weapons
     - 2. _____
   - d. Dragging nets
     - 1. Fishing
2. _____
   - a. Arrowheads
   - b. _____
   - c. Knives
   - d. _____
3. Cane

C. STONES

1. _____
   - a. _____
     - 1. Farming
   - b. Axes
     - 1. Weapons
     - 2. _____
2. Ornamentation
3. _____

Answer Keys

Level One, Lesson 1: Did You Know ... ? (p. 6–13)
BEFORE READING
A.   Prereading Activity: Amazing Facts
Answers will vary.
B.   Vocabulary: Multiple Syllables
1. 4, mar • su • pi • al   2. 3, gen • tle • men
3. 3, vol • ca • noes   4. 4, tem • per • a • ture
5. 3, fol • li • cle   6. 3, de • pend • ing
7. 3, es • ti • mate   8. 3, sci • en • tists
9. 4, pop • u • la • tion   10. 3, e • rup • tions
C.   Prereading Questions
1. fascinating facts   2a–b. Answers will vary.
3. about some fascinating facts.
AFTER READING
1a.   She has no eyebrows.
  b.   straight - round; wavy - oval; curly - square
  c.   girls by 0.5%   d. nerve endings
2a.   Answers will vary.
  b.   counted them or estimated them
  c.   Answers will vary.
  d.   A human body needs water for its bones, brain, and other organs.
3a–b.   Answers will vary.
ASSESSMENT/REINFORCEMENT
B.   Crossword Puzzle

Level One, Lesson 2: Deep Sea Squid (p. 14–20)
BEFORE READING
A.   Prereading Activity: True or False?
1. F   2. F   3. T   4. F   5. T
6. T   7. F   8. F   9. F   10. T
B.   Vocabulary Meaning
1. Oahu   2. aquarium   3. tentacles
4. trolling   5. appendage
C.   Prereading Questions
1. squid   2a–b. Answers will vary.
3. about the deep sea squid.
AFTER READING
1a.   Its image was recorded.
  b.   In the Hawaiian Islands
  c.   ten appendages, two tentacles with suction cups, large floppy fins
  d.   Both "trap" their prey and then eat it.

2a.   Little is known about it; scientists haven't been able to examine it.
  b.   unusually long appendages that radiate from its body; elbow bends in the appendages; fins that look like big, floppy elephant ears
  c.   The deep sea squid has suction cups on its arms like a regular squid. It is different because it has ten equal appendages, it has bends in its arms, and it has fins.
3a.   They seem to be more unlike—at least in the way they look. Because it lives in deeper water.
  b.   Answers will vary.
  c.   1. body   2. fin   3. tentacle   4. arm
ASSESSMENT/REINFORCEMENT
D.   First Letter/Last Letter Puzzle
1. hang   2. Gulf of Mexico   3. Oahu
4. unclassified 5. deep   6. Pacific
7. cups   8. spider   9. reaches
10. spotted

Level One, Lesson 3: Delicious Mistakes (p. 21–28)
BEFORE READING
A.   Prereading Activity: Either/Or
1–3. Answers will vary.
B.   Vocabulary Synonyms: Answers will vary.
Some examples are:
Delicious: delectable, luscious, scrumptious, yummy
Pharmacist: druggist, chemist, apothecary
Accidental: random, unintentional, chance, incidental
C.   Prereading Questions
1. about foods invented by mistake
2a–b. Answers will vary.
3. how some foods were invented.
AFTER READING

1a.	Potato chips	Doughnut holes	Chocolate chip cookies	Brown 'n Serve Rolls
	1853	1885	1930	1949

  b.   because the inventor, Ruth Wakefield, invented them and served them at her Toll House Inn
  c.   Cakes tended to be soggy in the middle.
  d.   Florida
2a.   With intelligence and quick thinking, mistakes can result in delicious things.
  b.   Crum was mad and intending to seek revenge on his customer, but it backfired on him and became a hit.
  c.   A successful person views his or her mistake in a positive way; an unsuccessful person just looks at the negative side.
  d.   The recipe was brought to America from France by Thomas Jefferson.
3a –b. Answers will vary.

ASSESSMENT/REINFORCEMENT
Brand Names
1. Yes, M   2. Yes, K   3. No, F   4. Yes, I
5. No, B   6. Yes, L   7. Yes, H   8. Yes, A
9. Yes, N   10. Yes, C   11. Yes, E   12. Yes, J
13. No, D   14. No, G

Level Two, Lesson 1: Totally Absurd Inventions ... for Pets (p. 29–35)

BEFORE READING

A. Prereading Activity: Inventors and Their Inventions

1. c   2. a   3. e   4. b   5. d

B. Vocabulary: Definitions: Answers will vary. Some examples are:

1. meaningfully   2. almost entirely   3. get rid of
4. over and over   5. unusual; one of a kind
6. clever or sly
7. pierced with a row of holes to enable something to be torn easily   8. splendid
9. ordinary or commonplace
10. goods that are shipped

C. Prereading Questions

1.   inventors and inventions
2a–b. Answers will vary.
3.   about silly inventions for pets.

AFTER READING

1a. things, items, matter, material
  b. 1. absurd   2. goofy   3. wacky
  c. Doggie Luggage
  d. It eliminates the chore of petting and scratching your pet.
2a. Doggie Luggage
  b. The apparatus and plastic would probably trip the dog, or the dog would rip through the plastic as it ran.
  c. to go after or chase
  d. Answers will vary.
3a. a word that is used alone to express strong emotion; Bye-Bye!; Bon Voyage!; Later!
  b. Answers will vary.
  c. It would probably scratch too hard or in a bad place, harming the baby, or it could scare the baby.

Level Two, Lesson 2: Go for Broke! (p. 36–44)

A. Prereading Activity: Japanese in America in World War II

1–2. Answers will vary.

B. "Go for Broke!' Vocabulary

1–10. Answers will vary.

C. Prereading Questions

1.   World War II
2a–b. Answers will vary.
3.   what the title of the reading means.

AFTER READING

1a. a second-generation Japanese-American
  b. Texas soldiers who were lost in a forest in France.
  c. The government gathered all Japanese-Americans on the west coast and put them into internment camps.
  d. They suffered so many losses.
2a. The soldiers not only had to fight the enemy (Germans, Italians, and Japanese), but also had to fight discrimination from Americans.
  b. Answers will vary.
  c. They felt it was the only way they could prove their loyalty to America.
  d. They were shorter and weighed less.
3a. The Tuskegee Airmen; The Buffalo Soldiers; The Navajo Code Talkers

  b. Interview a veteran of the 442nd and write a story about these heroic soldiers for the newspaper. Ideas will vary.
  c. Answers will vary.
  d. Approximately 400,000

ASSESSMENT/REINFORCEMENT

There was **PREJUDICE** against Japanese-Americans even before the attack on **PEARL HARBOR**; however, after the attack, the prejudice greatly increased. Although the Japanese-Americans were loyal U.S. **CITIZENS**, many people feared they would side with **JAPAN**. As a result, the basic **HUMAN RIGHTS** of the Japanese-Americans were abused. Their homes were **SEARCHED** for cameras, radios, and weapons in the fear they would be used against the United States. They were assigned numbers and had to register with the **GOVERNMENT**. In 1942, President **ROOSEVELT** ordered the evacuation of Japanese-Americans from the west coast. They had to leave their homes to go to one of ten **INTERNMENT** camps in California, Colorado, Utah, Arkansas, and other states.

The government wanted everyone to believe that the Japanese-Americans accepted the **RELOCATION** as a wartime necessity. Although they did not want to leave their homes, the Japanese-Americans cooperated with the government to show their **LOYALTY** to their country.

The barracks at the internment camps were crowded and offered little **PRIVACY**. Each family had a small space in which to live, with a single light bulb providing the only light. They slept on cots. The camps were surrounded by **BARBED WIRE** and **GUARDS**.

After about a year, the Japanese-Americans were allowed to go home. Unfortunately, many of their homes and farms had been **DESTROYED**; their personal **PROPERTY** and possessions were gone. They had to begin again, looking for **JOBS** and **HOUSING**. No Japanese-Americans were ever convicted or accused of **SPYING** or **TREASON** during World War II. In fact, 33,000 Japanese-Americans served in the **ARMED FORCES**; two of the most **DECORATED** units in the war were Japanese-American.

In 1980, a government commission reported that the internment of Japanese-Americans was due to "race prejudice, war hysteria, and a **FAILURE** of political leadership." The government apologized, and the surviving Japanese-Americans were each given a **PAYMENT** of $20,000.

Level Two, Lesson 3: Bill of Rights, Part I (p. 45–52)

BEFORE READING

A. Prereading Activity: What Do You Think?

1. Yes. Double jeopardy says the criminal can't be tried in the same <u>court</u> twice.
2. Yes. This is not covered under freedom of religion because not seeking medical help constitutes a clear danger to the child.
3. No, the Ku Klux Klan has freedom of speech, as long as the cross is erected in a <u>public</u> square where other forms of free speech are practiced.

B. Vocabulary: Word Meaning

Part I: Alphabetical Order

acquit, amend, arbitrary, eminent, incriminate, indicted, irrelevant, jeopardy, prosecute, ratify

Part II: Synonyms: Answers will vary.

C. Prereading Questions

1. The Bill of Rights   2a–b.   Answers will vary.
    c. about the Bill of Rights.

AFTER READING

1a. because they thought the Constitution made the federal government too powerful

 b. a delegate to the Constitutional Convention who wanted a "bill of rights" to protect its citizens

 c. Virginia Declaration of Rights; Declaration of Independence; Magna Carta; Articles of Confederation; English Bill of Rights

 d. The Third Amendment—this practice ceased with the end of the American Revolution.

 e. 1. First Amendment   2. Fifth Amendment
     3. First Amendment   4. Fourth Amendment
     5. Fifth Amendment   6. Second Amendment

2a. It outlines their basic rights.

 b. No one can be tried twice in the same court for the same crime. It prevents authorities from continuing to prosecute someone who has been acquitted.

 c. He or she is refusing to testify. The Fifth Amendment prohibits a person from having to testify against himself or herself.

3a–b. Answers will vary.

ASSESSMENT/REINFORCEMENT

1. F
2. T
3. F
4. F
5. T
6. T
7. F
8. F
9. T
10. F

Level Two, Lesson 4: Bill of Rights, Part II (p. 53–60)
BEFORE READING

A. Prereading Activity: What Do You Think?

1. Fourth Amendment: Cannot be arrested without a warrant; without protection of his basic rights; right to privacy in his own home
    Sixth Amendment: Should have been informed of the nature and cause of the accusations

2. Sixth Amendment: Right to an attorney; cannot be jailed for an unnecessary length of time

3. Eighth Amendment: Excessive bail cannot be charged

4. Fifth Amendment: Does not have to testify against himself
    Eighth Amendment: Excessive fines cannot be imposed.

B. Vocabulary: Word Meaning

Part I: Alphabetical Order

accuser, electrocute, guarantee, humane, inquisitions, lethal, monetary, pivotal, reiterates, scope

Part II: Synonyms: Answers will vary.

C. Prereading Questions

1. more about the Bill of Rights

2a–b. Answers will vary.

3. more about the Bill of Rights.

AFTER READING

1a. The Bill of Rights establishes basic American civil liberties that the federal government cannot violate; defines the scope of individual freedom; and insures a democratic government.

2a. the right to be informed of the nature and cause of the accusations; right to an attorney; cannot be jailed for an unnecessary length of time; excessive bail cannot be charged; right to a speedy and public trial; right to face his accuser

 b. Prisoners cannot be tortured to death, but may be electrocuted, gassed, shot by a firing squad, or given a lethal injection.

 c. It was added to reduce the fears that the "new" national government might someday seek to exceed its proper power.

3a–c. Answers will vary.

ASSESSMENT/REINFORCEMENT

B. Bill of Rights

First Amendment: Freedom of speech, Freedom of the press, Freedom of religion, Freedom of association and assembly

Second Amendment: Right to bear arms

Third Amendment: Protection against being forced to house soldiers

Fourth Amendment: Guards against unreasonable search and seizure, Cannot be jailed without protection of basic rights, Right to privacy and personal security, Cannot be arrested without a warrant

Fifth Amendment: Cannot be prosecuted until indicted by a grand jury, Double jeopardy, Self-incrimination, Due process of law, Eminent domain

Sixth Amendment: Right to be informed of the nature and cause of the accusation, Right to a speedy and public trial, Right to an attorney

Seventh Amendment: Right to a jury trial for monetary damages in federal court

Eighth Amendment: Prohibits use of cruel or unusual punishment; Prevents excessive bail being charged

Ninth Amendment: Rights to life, liberty, and the pursuit of happiness

Tenth Amendment: Powers not assigned to the federal government are held by the states or the people

Level Three, Lesson 1: Baseball's Hall of Fame (p. 61–67)
BEFORE READING

A. Prereading Activity: Baseball Word Search

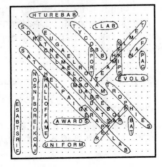

B. Hall of Fame Vocabulary

1–6. Sentences and definitions will vary; some definition examples are:
1. tourist - a person who travels for pleasure to places of interest
2. artifact - a simple object representing a culture
3. picturesque - calling forth a striking mental picture
4. repository - a place where something is stored
5. plaque - a thin piece of metal, wood, etc., inscribed to commemorate a person's accomplishment, an event, building, etc.
6. memorabilia - things worth remembering; a collection of souvenirs

C. Prereading Questions

1. baseball
2a–b. Answers will vary.
3. about Baseball's Hall of Fame.

AFTER READING

1a. The National Baseball Hall of Fame
 b. Cooperstown, New York
 c. Most Americans have played or watched baseball; baseball is a national pastime.
2a. Preserve history: by collecting baseball artifacts
 Honor excellence: inducting players into the Hall of Fame Gallery
 Connect generations: families share common knowledge about baseball
 b. It means that "official" and authentic treasures are in the Hall of Fame.
 c. umpires, Negro League players, owners, managers
3a. Answers will vary.
 b. Eckersley played for Oakland; Molitor played for Milwaukee, Toronto, and Minnesota.

ASSESSMENT/REINFORCEMENT

The All-American Girls Professional Baseball League

1. Rockford Peaches, Kenosha Comets, Racine Belles, South Bend Blue Sox, Milwaukee Chicks, Minneapolis Millerettes
2. If the public recognized the managers' names, they would be more likely to be interested in attending the games and take the league more seriously.
3. With a few exceptions, the AAGPBL games were being played with the same general rules as in the men's major leagues. There were variations in the distances between bases, the distance from the pitching mound to home plate, the size of the ball, and pitching styles. Over the years, modifications were made to the original distances and equipment; pitching changed from underhand to overhand.
4. Check the website for a complete list. The gist was to always appear attractive and properly attired, no smoking or drinking in public, checking in with chaperones, curfew, no fraternizing with the different teams, etc.
5. They were fined money for breaking the rules.
6. So they would be suitably attired, use proper etiquette, and project a positive and attractive image to the public to avoid negative publicity for the League.
7. Cleansing cream, lipstick, rouge, deodorant, mild astringent, face powder, hand lotion, and a depilatory.

8. The expression "girl next door" means someone wholesome and attractive; someone you would like to have living next door.
9. The uniforms consisted of a short-skirted flared tunic, similar to the figure skating costumes of that time. Satin tights, knee-high baseball socks, and a baseball hat completed the uniform.
10. Each city's team uniform was a different color and had its own symbolic patch on the front.
11. The two teams at each game formed a "V" for Victory from home plate down the first and third baselines, followed by the playing of the "Star-Spangled Banner."
12. The players played exhibition games to support the Red Cross and the armed forces and also visited wounded veterans at army hospitals.
13. Over 600 women athletes
14. To be as friendly and as gracious as possible when giving autographs and answering questions
15. Eventually there was no centralized control of the League, the teams lost their franchises, local fan bases declined due to the availability of other types of recreation and entertainment, and major league games were televised.

Level Three, Lesson 2: Habitat for Humanity (p. 68–75)

BEFORE READING

A. Prereading Activity: Homelessness

Answers will vary. Hopefully, at least one student will mention Habitat for Humanity, and then you can determine what students know about it.

B. Vocabulary: A Matter of Phrasing

1. locally available - materials found nearby
2. partnership housing - people in need work side-by-side with volunteers to build simple, decent homes
3. affordable housing - houses that people with low incomes can afford
4. grass-roots movement - action from common people
5. a matter of conscience - to do the right thing
6. construction costs - the cost of the materials and labor to construct a house
7. modestly sized - not big and not small
8. handicap-accessible - a place that is set up so the handicapped can easily access it
9. no-interest loan - organizations that loan the money will not make money on the loan
10. biblical scholar - a learned person who specializes in the study of the Bible

C. Prereading Questions

1. Habitat for Humanity   2a–b. Answers will vary.
 c. about Habitat for Humanity.

AFTER READING

1a. Linda and Millard Fuller and Clarence Jordan
 b. to build simple, decent, affordable housing for those who need it
 c. the future homeowners and their family
 d. volunteers and homeowners work, materials are donated, no-interest loans are granted
2a. Habitat for Humanity is a positive, concrete method for fighting homelessness.
 b. Yes, because they will have more of an investment of time and labor in the outcome and will appreciate the work that went into it.

3a–c. Answers will vary.

ASSESSMENT/REINFORCEMENT

Habitat for Humanity Criss-Cross Puzzle

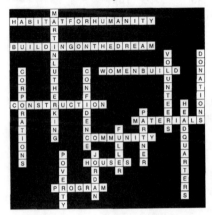

Level Three, Lesson 3: Harlem USA (p. 76–84)

BEFORE READING

A.   Prereading Activity: What I Think I Know

1. Answers should all be checked.

B.   Vocabulary: Two-Word Phrases

1. chief artery - main intersection
2. known internationally - famous outside the country
3. transportation facilities - means of transportation
4. financial panic - fear about the loss or lack of money
5. intellectual atmosphere - an air of serious discussion
6. orchestra seats - the section of a theater near the orchestra
7. ethnic groups - people whose native origins differ
8. decrepit dwellings - buildings and/or housing in very bad repair
9. residential mobility - moving from one place to another
10. severe deterioration - very bad state of repair

C.   Prereading Questions

1.   the city of Harlem

2a–b. Answers wil vary.

3.   about Harlem.

AFTER READING

1a. neighborhood   b. 125th Street
 c. Irish   d. True, True

2a. overcrowding, unemployment, deterioration of dwellings

 b. Yes. Property can be repaired, jobs created, middle-class people could move in.

 c. The Renaissance was a historical period of rebirth of interest in art and culture. The Harlem Renaissance was a rebirth in African-American art and culture that occurred in Harlem.

3a. Answers will vary.

 b. clashing cultures, cycle of poverty, unemployment, under-educated youth

 c. Answers will vary. The poem could be about racism. Hughes meditates on the exclusion of blacks from the American Dream and the possible outlets for their feelings of anger and frustration.

ASSESSMENT/REINFORCEMENT

Singers, Actors, Comedians: Bert Williams, George Walker, Aida Overton Walker, Florence Mills, Ethel Waters, Billie Holliday, Louis Armstrong

Poets, Novelists: W.E.B. DuBois, Zora Neale Hurston, Langston Hughes, Ralph Ellison, Jessie Fauset, Claude McKay, Countee Cullen

Politicians: Fiorello H. LaGuardia, Marcus Garvey, Adam Clayton Powell, Jr.

Lawyer, Judge: Hurbert T. Delaney

Musicians: Count Basie, Duke Ellington, Louis Armstrong, Luis Russell, Pops Foster, Fletcher Henderson

Artists: Augusta Savage, Aaron Douglas, Jacob Lawrence

Educators: Charles S. Johnson, E. Franklin Frazier, W.E.B. DuBois

Photographer: James Van Der Zee

Medical Doctor: Louis T. Wright

Level Three, Lesson 4: The Gentle Giant (p. 85–92)

BEFORE READING

A.   Prereading Activity: Building Bridges

 Answers will vary. It is a statue of Robert Pershing Wadlow.

B.   Vocabulary: Antonyms - Giant Vocabulary

Answers will vary. Some examples are:

a. short	b. easy	c. disadvantage
d. smaller	e. coward	f. lethargic
g. right	h. daughter	i. dream
j. running	k. ill will	l. mother
m. stand	n. create	o. mean
p. impulsive	q. rough	r. loud
s. old	t. insult	

C.   Prereading Questions

1.   giants   2a–b. Answers will vary.

3.   who the Gentle Giant is.

AFTER READING

1a. Answers will vary.

 b. too tall for car; difficulty in attending college; bad feet

 c. He got blisters on his feet without knowing it because he had little sensation in his feet. The blisters became infected.

 d. the International Shoe Company

2a. He was regarded as a "freak," and nothing was made big enough for him.

 b. Doctors could probably "cure" or slow down the growth process.

 c. a person who promotes a company or a cause

 d. Answers will vary.

3a–b. Answers will vary.

 c. 22 years old   d. Answers will vary.

ASSESSMENT/REINFORCEMENT

B.   Robert Wadlow's Life

 Chronological order: 5, 12, 3, 9, 1, 2, 11, 10, 7, 8, 6, 4

Level Four, Lesson 1: Life in the Desert (p. 93–101)
BEFORE READING
A. Prereading Activity: Exploring What Is Known
     Drawings will vary.
B. Vocabulary: Which Word Fits?
1. rodent   2. tropical   3. nocturnal
4. ingested   5. frigid   6. barren
7. pistachio   8. addax
C. Prereading Questions
1. Answers will vary.   2a–b. Answers will vary.
3. what lives in a desert.
AFTER READING
1a. 5: to, of, in, at, during; *of* is used most often.
  b. poisonous
  c. Apache plume, Arizona poppy, desert paintbrush, desert lily, devil's claw, datura
  d. pores
2a. Deserts are barren regions that support very little plant and animal life; what life there is has adapted to the conditions of the desert.
  b. A Gila monster is a large, slow-moving, poisonous lizard. Maybe when people first saw this giant lizard they called it a monster, or something similar.
  c. spreading out over a large area; ivy, weeds, housing developments, cities
  d. Answers will vary. *Perennial* means lasting or active year after year.
3a. Answers will vary.
  b. Drawings will vary.
ASSESSMENT/REINFORCEMENT
B. Fill in the Blanks: Life in the Desert
     Wild animals and plants have **adapted** for **survival** in the deserts of the world. **People** have also learned how to live in the deserts. People of the desert usually live in small family groups, or **tribes**. They are often **nomadic**—that is, they travel in search of **water**, game, and forage for their animals. They camp in one particular spot for only as long as the area's limited **resources** will **support** them. These wanderers are called **Bedouins** in North Africa and **Bushmen** in Australia. Some of the **Mongols** of Central Asia are also nomadic. In the Americas, various **Indian** tribes chose the desert as a place to live. This may have been as a defense against other tribes who **inhabited** the lusher biomes of the area. In the deserts of the **southwestern** United States, we find the Pueblo, Navajo, **Apache**, and Papago Indians.
     Modern people are moving into the desert biomes. Desert sands can grow good crops if **water** can be made available. This is done through **irrigation** canals and deeply drilled wells. Some desert regions are also rich in **minerals** such as gold, silver, and **copper. Mining** activities utilize large tracts of desert lands, as does the **grazing** of domestic livestock. Some **cacti** have become collectors' items and are disappearing from their natural **environment**.
     Some desert land should be set aside for the future, so endangered desert species will be able to **survive**. Some of these **endangered** species are the desert bighorn ram, the kit fox, and the Gila monster.

Level Four, Lesson 2: Tuskegee Airmen (p. 102–109)
BEFORE READING
Prereading Activity: Tuskegee University
1. Tuskegee University   2. 1881
3. Booker T. Washington   4. Tuskegee, Alabama
5. the first black fighter pilots
6. "He lifted the veil of ignorance from his people and painted the way to progress through education and industry."
7. Dr. Benjamin F. Payton (2004)
8. 3,000 (as of this printing)
9. 5,000 acres; 70 buildings
10. Campbell, a politician, asked Adams, a former slave, what it would take to get the black vote. Adams wanted education, and Campbell, who got the black vote, made it happen.
B. Vocabulary: Adjectives
What Is ... ?
1. a fighter pilot - a pilot who fights enemy aircraft
2. a black pilot - an African-American pilot
3. a combat pilot - a pilot who flies in combat
4. a military pilot - a pilot flying for the U.S. Armed Forces
5. a segregated air unit - an all-white or all-black aviation unit
6. an aeronautical engineering program - a course of study to learn about aviation
7. a technical course - a course intended to teach someone how to do something
8. aviation training - training in aeronautics
9. a major political force - someone or something that can influence policy
10. a credible reputation - positive and respected reputation
C. Prereading Questions
1.   airline pilots
2a–b. Answers will vary.
3.   who the Tuskegee Airmen are.
AFTER READING
1a. the first black pilots to qualify as military pilots
  b. good location, good reputation, good beginning program
  c. "... a veritable cathedral of practical learning and black self-help."
  d. combat in the air
2a. Black military pilots made an important contribution to winning World War II.
  b. They weren't considered "smart enough."
  c. pilots, flight engineers, gunners, mechanics, armorers, navigators, bombardiers
  d. They did not lose even one bomber they were escorting.
3a. positive, successful, earned the respect of the military, and opened doors of opportunity for African-Americans
  b. Yes, they were put into a segregated unit.
  c. Answers will vary.

ASSESSMENT/REINFORCEMENT
B.   Tuskegee Airmen: Criss-Cross Puzzle:

Level Four, Lesson 3: The Choctaw (p.110–118)
BEFORE READING
B.   Vocabulary Meaning

1. fatigued (fə • tēgd′) - tired

2. encampment (ĕn • kămp′ • mənt) - a camp or campsite

3. assimilate (ə • sĭm′ • ə • lāt′) - to absorb information into the mind or body

4. unscrupulous (ŭn • skrōō′ • pyə • ləs) - contemptuous of what is right

5. enterprise (ĕnt′ • ər • prīz′) - an undertaking with complications and risk

6. endeavor (ĕn • dĕv′ • ər) - an earnest attempt

C.   Prereading Questions
1.   Native Americans
2a–b.   Answers will vary.
3.   about the Choctaw people.

AFTER READING
1a.   It was a good place to find and raise food.
 b.   Toscalusa
 c.   about 7,000, which was only about 25% of the entire Nation
 d.   Chief Gregory E. Pyle, since 1997 (as of this printing)
2a.   White businessmen and farmers wanted it.
 b.   Missionaries helped them, and they were not a hostile tribe.
 c.   to celebrate their cultural heritage; to unite families
3a–b. Answers will vary.
  c.   Answers will vary. Some examples include: actors Graham Greene and Chief Dan George; musicians Carlos Nakai and Ronnie Robertson; ballet dancer Maria Talchief; politician Wilma Mankiller.

ASSESSMENT/REINFORCEMENT
B.   Native Americans: Living Off the Land

Forest/Plains

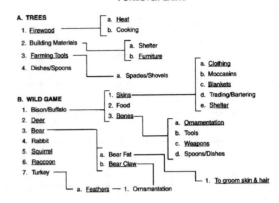

FORESTS/PLAINS

In or Along Rivers and Streams

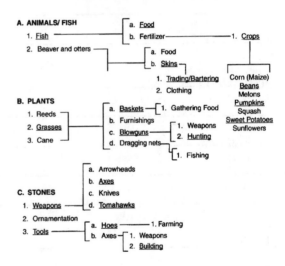

IN OR ALONG RIVERS AND STREAMS

Teacher Notes

MONDAY: _____
_____
_____
_____
_____

TUESDAY: _____
_____
_____
_____
_____

WEDNESDAY: _____
_____
_____
_____
_____

THURSDAY: _____
_____
_____
_____
_____

FRIDAY: _____
_____
_____
_____
_____